Steck-Vaughn

BOOK 1

WORLD HISTORY and YOU

Vivian Bernstein

Consultant
Karen Tindel Wiggins
Director of Social Studies
Richardson Independent School District
Richardson, Texas

STECK-VAUGHN
C O M P A N Y
ELEMENTARY • SECONDARY • ADULT • LIBRARY

ABOUT THE AUTHOR

Vivian Bernstein is the author of *America's Story*, *America's History: Land of Liberty*, *World Geography and You*, *American Government*, and *Decisions for Health*. She received her Master of Arts degree from New York University. Bernstein is active with professional organizations in social studies, education, and reading. She gives presentations to school faculties and professional groups about content area reading. Bernstein was a teacher in the New York City Public School System for a number of years.

ACKNOWLEDGMENTS

Executive Editor: Diane Sharpe
Senior Editor: Martin S. Saiewitz
Project Editor: Meredith Edgley

Design Manager: Rusty Kaim
Photo Editor: Margie Foster
Electronic Production: JoAnn Estrada, Jill Klinger

CREDITS

Cover Photography: (Sphinx, Great Wall) © Index Stock, (ship) © Marco Corsetti/FPG, (map) © Superstock

p.3 © Giraudon/Art Resource; p.4 © Tom Bean/Tony Stone Images; p.6 (top) © J. Kostich/Leo de Wys, (bottom) © John Reader/Photo Researchers; p.10 © David Sutherland/Tony Stone Images; p.11 (top) © Fridmar Damm/Leo de Wys, (bottom) The Granger Collection; p.12 (top) The Bettmann Archive, (left) The Granger Collection; p.13 (top) North Wind Picture Archive, (left) The Granger Collection; p.14 (top) © Eric J. Lessing/Art Resource, (bottom) The Granger Collection; p.17 © Ronald Sheridan Photo Library/Ancient Art & Architecture Collection; p.18 The Granger Collection; p.19 (top, middle) The Granger Collection, (bottom) © Giraudon/Art Resource; p.22 North Wind Picture Archive; p.23 © Lance Nelson/The Stock Market; p.24 (top) North Wind Picture Archive, (left) The Granger Collection; p.25 (top) © Mark Harris/Tony Stone Images, (bottom) The Granger Collection; p.29 © Dilip Mehta/Contact Press Images/The Stock Market; p.30 © Scala/Art Resource; p.31 (top) © Superstock, (bottom) © Victoria & Albert Museum, London/Art Resource; p.32 (top) © Ric Ergenbright Photography, (left) The Bettmann Archive; p.35 © Superstock; p.36 © China Stock/Yang Xiuyun; p.37 (top) © Giraudon/Art Resource, (middle) © Ronald Sheridan Photo Library/Ancient Art & Architecture Collection, (bottom) The Granger Collection; p.38 (top) © Giraudon/Art Resource, (middle) © Superstock, (bottom) The Granger Collection; p.39 The Granger Collection; p.43 © Superstock; p.44 © J. Messerschmidt/Leo de Wys; p.45 The Granger Collection; p.46 (top) The Granger Collection, (left) © Ronald Sheridan Photo Library/Ancient Art & Architecture Collection; p.47 (top, bottom) North Wind Picture Archive, (middle) Archive Photos; p.48 (top) North Wind Picture Archive, (middle) The Granger Collection, (bottom) © Michele Burgess/The Stock Market; p.49 (both) The Granger Collection; p.52 © Superstock; p.53 (top) © Eric J. Lessing/Art Resource, (left) © Scala/Art Resource; p.54 (top) North Wind Picture Archive, (middle) © Scala/Art Resource, (bottom) The Granger Collection; p.55 The Granger Collection; p.56 (top) © Larry Mulvehill/Photo Researchers, (middle) © Scala/Art Resource, (bottom) The Granger Collection; p.60 The Granger Collection; p.61 (top) The Bettmann Archive, (middle) © Oudna/Ronald Sheridan Photo Library/Ancient Art & Architecture Collection, (bottom) The Granger Collection; p.63 (top) The Granger Collection, (bottom) © Scala/Art Resource; p.64 The Granger Collection; p.67 © Scala Art Resource; p.68 (top, bottom) The Granger Collection, (middle) © Eric J. Lessing/Art Resource; p.71 The Granger Collection; p.72 (top) The Bettmann Archive, (bottom) The Granger Collection; p.73 © Steve Vidler/Leo de Wys; p.76 © Fridmar Damm/Leo de Wys; p.77 The Granger Collection; p.78 (top) © J. Cassio/Leo de Wys, (middle, bottom) The Granger Collection; p.79 (top) © Mehmet Biber/Photo Researchers, (left) The Granger Collection; p.82 Stock Montage; p.83 (top, bottom) The Granger Collection, (middle) North Wind Picture Archive; p.84 © China Stock; p.85 (top) North Wind Picture Archive, (middle) © David Lawrence/The Stock Market, (bottom) The Granger Collection; p.86 (top) © Fridmar Damm/Leo de Wys, (bottom) The Bettmann Archive; p.91 © Scala/Art Resource; p.92 © The Pierpont Morgan Library/Art Resource; p.93 (middle) North Wind Picture Archive, (bottom) © Giraudon/Art Resource; p.94 (both) The Granger Collection; p.95 (top) The Bettmann Archive, (middle) The Granger Collection, (bottom) © Superstock; p.98 The Bettmann Archive; p.99 (top) The Bettmann Archive, (middle) North Wind Picture Archive, (bottom) The Granger Collection; p.100 (both) North Wind Picture Archive; p.101 (top) © Superstock, (bottom) North Wind Picture Archive; p.104 © Art Resource; p.105 (top) © Superstock, (middle, bottom) The Granger Collection; p.106 (top) The Granger Collection, (middle, bottom) © Scala/Art Resource; p.107 (top) The Granger Collection, (middle) © Superstock, (bottom) Stock Montage; p.108 © Superstock; p.111 The Granger Collection; p.112 (top) The Granger Collection, (bottom) © Scala/Art Resource; p.113 (left, right) The Granger Collection, (middle) The Bettmann Archive; p.114 (top, middle) North Wind Picture Archive, (bottom) The Granger Collection; p.117 © Superstock; p.118 The Granger Collection; p.119 (top, middle) The Granger Collection, (bottom) © Eric J. Lessing/Art Resource; p.120 (top, middle) The Granger Collection, (bottom) North Wind Picture Archive; p.124 © Superstock; p.125 © Brian Seed/Tony Stone Images; p.126 © Lee Boltin Picture Library; p.127 (top) © George Holton/Photo Researchers, (bottom) North Wind Picture Archive; p.128 (top) © Cynthia Ellis, (middle) The Granger Collection, (bottom) © Harvey Lloyd/Gamma Liaison; p.129 The Granger Collection; p.132 Stock Montage; p.133 (both) The Granger Collection; p.134 (top) Archive Photos, (bottom) The Granger Collection; p.135 (top) North Wind Picture Archive, (left) The Bettmann Archive; pp.139, 140, 141 The Granger Collection; p.142 (top) The Granger Collection, (bottom) National Portrait Gallery/Smithsonian Institution; p.143 (top) The Granger Collection; p.144 (top, bottom) The Granger Collection; pp.146, 148 The Granger Collection; p.149 (top) North Wind Picture Archive, (bottom) The Granger Collection; p.150 (top) The Granger Collection, (bottom) The Bettmann Archive; p.151 (top) North Wind Picture Archive, (left) The Granger Collection; p.152 (top) The Bettmann Archive, (bottom) © Superstock; p.155 North Wind Picture Archive; p.157 (top) The Bettmann Archive, (left) Archive Photos; p.158 Hulton Deutsch; p.159 (top) The Bettmann Archive, (left) North Wind Picture Archive; pp.162, 163, 164 The Granger Collection; p.167 © Schalkwijk/Art Resource; p.168 (top) The Bettmann Archive, (middle, bottom) The Granger Collection; p.169 (top, bottom) The Bettmann Archive, (middle) The Granger Collection; p.170 The Granger Collection; p.171 The Bettmann Archive.

ISBN 0-8172-6325-X

5 6 7 8 9 PO 99 98

Contents

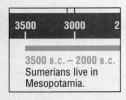

3500   3000   2
3500 B.C. – 2000 B.C.
Sumerians live in
Mesopotamia.

People in History

List of Maps

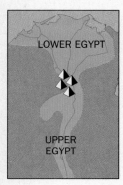

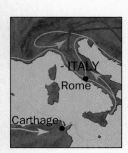

List of Skill Builders

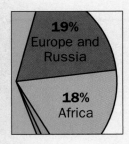

Charts, Graphs, and Diagrams

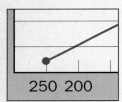

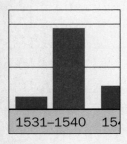

To the Reader

You are about to read an exciting story about the world. As you read *World History and You*, you will learn how people started the first cities and why many early civilizations disappeared. You will learn why wars have been fought everywhere in the world.

Your study of world history will begin by traveling back in time for thousands of years. The earliest people spent most of their time just finding enough food to eat. Later, after people learned how to grow food, they began to live in villages and cities. As one civilization conquered another, empires were formed. Great religions began. Important ideas developed and spread.

World History and You will help you become a better social studies student. Start by learning the vocabulary words for each chapter. Try to review vocabulary words from earlier chapters. Study each map and think about the ways geography can change the history of a place. Then read the text of each chapter carefully. By reading the chapter a second time, you will improve your understanding of history. Complete the chapter activities carefully, and your skills in writing and social studies will improve.

As you study world history, you will learn about men and women who changed the world they lived in. You will discover how past events have created the world we have today. You will learn about mistakes people made in the past. By learning from past mistakes, you can work for a better tomorrow. As you begin your journey into world history, remember that you, too, are part of the story.

Vivian Bernstein

Unit 1   The Ancient World

It is easy for us to know what happened ten years ago. People wrote in books, newspapers, and magazines about what was happening then. But 10,000 years ago, people did not yet know how to write. It is very difficult for us to know about people's lives 10,000 years ago.

We can learn about people of long ago from bones, tools, and other items we have found in the earth. Bones help us know what the first people looked like. We can tell how old the bones are and when these people lived. Tools from long ago tell us how people hunted or farmed. About 5,000 years ago, some people began to write their language on pieces of wet clay. We can learn more about people who wrote on clay than about earlier people who did not write.

Bones, stones, and clay have helped us learn about the problems people had long ago. One big problem was finding enough food and water. Many of the bones of people of long ago have been found near rivers. We believe that people lived near rivers because there was more food there than in places without water.

What was life like for people of long ago? Who built the first villages? What other items did people leave behind that help us learn

PACIFIC OCEAN

ATLANTIC OCEAN

PACIFIC OCEAN

INDIAN OCEAN

about their history? As you read Unit 1, think about the ways the people of long ago solved their problems. Think about why rivers were important to these early people. Read about the ideas the ancient world gave to us.

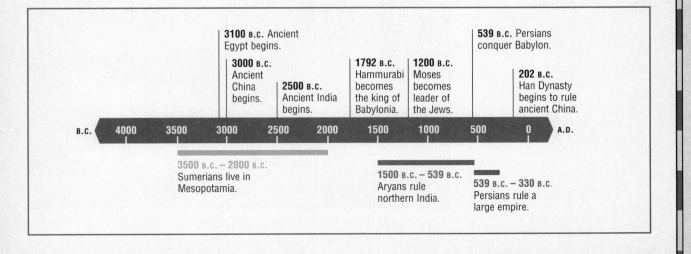

3100 B.C. Ancient Egypt begins.

3000 B.C. Ancient China begins.

2500 B.C. Ancient India begins.

1792 B.C. Hammurabi becomes the king of Babylonia.

1200 B.C. Moses becomes leader of the Jews.

539 B.C. Persians conquer Babylon.

202 B.C. Han Dynasty begins to rule ancient China.

| B.C. | 4000 | 3500 | 3000 | 2500 | 2000 | 1500 | 1000 | 500 | 0 | A.D. |

3500 B.C. – **2000** B.C. Sumerians live in Mesopotamia.

1500 B.C. – **539** B.C. Aryans rule northern India.

539 B.C. – **330** B.C. Persians rule a large empire.

CHAPTER 1

The First People

The first people did not live the way we live today. They did not grow food or live in houses. They did not read or write. In this chapter we will learn how the first people lived.

Archaeologists help us learn about people of long ago. Archaeologists are men and women who dig into the **earth**. They find and study the bones of people who lived thousands of years ago. The bones tell how people of long ago looked and how they lived. Archaeologists have also found animal bones from long ago. Some of these bones were used as **tools** for hunting.

Archaeologists have found tools used by people who lived during the **Stone Age**. It is called the Stone Age because most of the tools were made of stone. Stone tools lasted longer and were stronger than tools made of bone or wood. The Stone Age began more than 2,000,000 years ago. It ended about

THINK ABOUT AS YOU READ

1. How did the first people live?
2. What started the agricultural revolution?
3. Why did Stone Age farmers live near rivers?

NEW WORDS

♦ archaeologists
♦ earth
♦ tools
♦ Stone Age
♦ agricultural revolution
♦ tame

PEOPLE & PLACES

♦ Stone Age people

An archaeologist works slowly and carefully to remove old bones and tools from the earth.

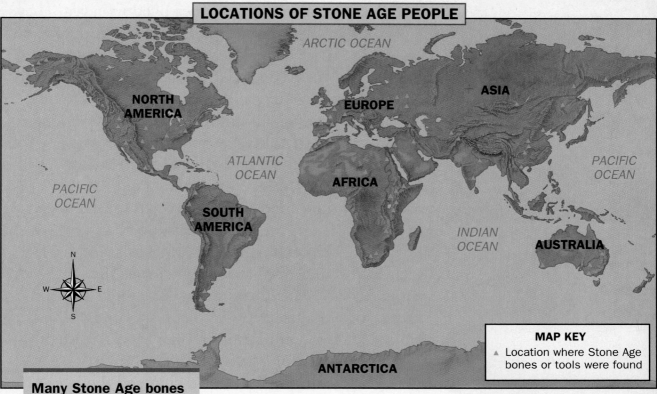

LOCATIONS OF STONE AGE PEOPLE

ARCTIC OCEAN

NORTH AMERICA

EUROPE

ASIA

ATLANTIC OCEAN

AFRICA

PACIFIC OCEAN

PACIFIC OCEAN

SOUTH AMERICA

INDIAN OCEAN

AUSTRALIA

MAP KEY
▲ Location where Stone Age bones or tools were found

ANTARCTICA

Many Stone Age bones and tools have been found near rivers. Where are some of these rivers located?

5,000 years ago. The people who lived then are called Stone Age people.

For thousands of years, Stone Age people spent most of their time looking for food. They did not know how to grow food. They found wild berries and nuts to eat. Most people were hunters. They killed animals for food. They made clothes from animal skins. Sometimes they made tools from animal bones.

People of the Stone Age learned to use fire. Fire gave heat and light. Stone Age people used fire to help them cook food and keep warm. Fire also kept people safe. Dangerous animals stayed away from fire at night.

For thousands of years, Stone Age people moved from place to place looking for food. They stayed in one place as long as there was food. When they could no longer find food, they moved to another place. They usually stayed near rivers. There were more animals and plants near rivers. Most Stone Age people moved many times. They did not build houses.

Cave painting from the Stone Age

Stone Age tool

Stone Age people sometimes lived in caves. They built fires in their caves to keep warm. Some people knew how to paint pictures. They made pictures on the walls of their caves. We can learn more about Stone Age people from the pictures they painted.

After thousands and thousands of years, Stone Age people learned how to grow their own food. This was the start of the **agricultural revolution**. The agricultural revolution was a change in the way people got their food. People learned to plant seeds to grow fruits and vegetables for food.

People became farmers. As time passed, they grew more and more food. Sometimes they grew enough food to feed wild animals. People began to **tame** dogs, goats, sheep, and cows. Some of these animals helped families with their work. Sometimes people killed the animals for food.

The agricultural revolution changed the lives of Stone Age people. Stone Age farmers did not have to move from place to place to hunt animals. They could live in one place. They lived on small farms. Some people built small mud houses on their farms. Sometimes people built their homes close together in small villages. Then they could work together and learn from each other.

Stone Age farmers needed water to grow food. Many times there was not enough rain. Farmers began to build their farms near rivers. They used river water to grow food.

As time passed, Stone Age people learned better ways to grow food. They made better stone tools. Stone Age people did not know how to make metal tools. They did not know how to read or write. After many years people in some parts of the world began to do these things. You will read about some of these people in the next chapters.

Using Vocabulary

Finish Up   Choose the word or words in dark print to best complete each sentence. Write the word or words on the correct blank line.

tamed   **tools**   **archaeologists**   **agricultural**   **Stone Age**

1. Men and women who study old bones to learn about people of long ago are called _____ .

2. Stone Age _____ were items that were used for hunting or farming.

3. The _____ was a period of millions of years in which most people used stones or animal bones to make tools.

4. The _____ revolution was a change in the way Stone Age people got their food.

5. Stone Age farmers _____ wild animals by giving them food to make them less afraid.

Read and Remember

Write the Answer   Write one or more sentences to answer each question.

1. When was the Stone Age? _____

   _____

2. How did Stone Age people use the animals they killed? _____

   _____

3. How did fire help Stone Age people? _____

   _____

4. Why did Stone Age people start their farms near rivers? _____

   _____

Skill Builder

Understanding Continents and Oceans We live on the planet **Earth**. Earth has large bodies of land called **continents**. There are seven continents. Earth also has four large bodies of water called **oceans**. The four oceans separate some of the

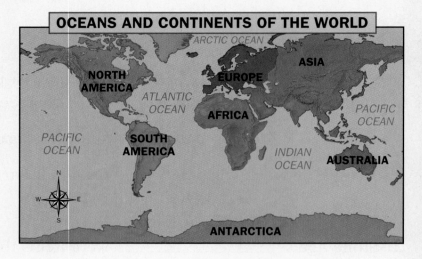

OCEANS AND CONTINENTS OF THE WORLD

continents. Look at the map. On a separate sheet of paper, list the four oceans and the seven continents. Then answer each question below.

1. Which two continents do not touch any other continents? _____

_____

2. Which ocean separates Africa and Australia? _____

3. Which five continents have coasts along the Atlantic Ocean? _____

_____

Using Map Directions The four main directions are **north, south, east,** and **west**. On maps these directions are shown by a **compass rose**. The compass rose shortens the directions to **N, S, E,** and **W**. Study the map above. Find the compass rose. Then finish each sentence with **north, south, east,** or **west**.

4. South America is _____ of Antarctica.

5. Africa is _____ of Europe.

6. The Pacific Ocean is _____ of Asia.

7. North America is _____ of the Atlantic Ocean.

Journal Writing

Write a short paragraph that tells how the agricultural revolution changed the lives of Stone Age people.

Crossword Puzzle

Each sentence below has a word missing. Choose the missing word for each sentence from the words in dark print. Then write the words in the correct places on the puzzle.

───────────────────── **ACROSS** ─────────────────────

hunters   painted   rivers   fire

1. Stone Age people _____ pictures on the walls of caves.

2. Stone Age people learned to get heat from _____ .

3. Many Stone Age people were animal _____ .

4. Farmers during the Stone Age built their farms near _____ .

───────────────────── **DOWN** ─────────────────────

earth   farmers   seeds   animals

5. Stone Age people tamed wild _____ .

6. Archaeologists dig in the _____ to find old bones and tools.

7. After the agricultural revolution, Stone Age _____ stopped moving from place to place.

8. Farmers planted _____ to grow fruits and vegetables.

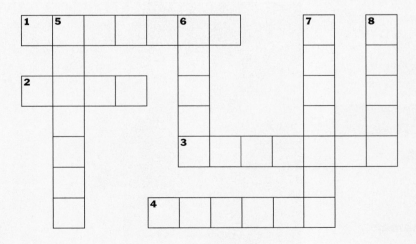

CHAPTER 2

People of Ancient Egypt

THINK ABOUT AS YOU READ

1. Why was ancient Egypt called "the gift of the Nile"?
2. How was ancient Egypt ruled?
3. Why did ancient Egyptians build pyramids and tombs?

NEW WORDS

- civilization
- fertile soil
- irrigate
- pharaohs
- god
- pyramids
- tombs
- slaves
- weapons
- temple

PEOPLE & PLACES

- ancient Egypt
- Nile River
- Egyptian
- Hatshepsut
- King Tutankhamen

Imagine how difficult it is to grow food in a land that is always hot and dry. The people of ancient Egypt faced that problem long ago. Egypt is a hot, dry land in Africa. It gets little rain. The Nile River flows through Egypt. More than 7,000 years ago, people in Africa learned to use water from the Nile River to grow food. As more people began to farm together along the Nile, they developed the **civilization** of ancient Egypt.

Egypt has been called "the gift of the Nile." This is because the Nile River prevented Egypt from being a huge desert. Without the Nile, people in ancient Egypt would not have been able to grow crops. The Nile made it possible for the civilization of ancient Egypt to last thousands of years.

The Nile is the longest river in the world. It is more than 4,150 miles long. Every summer in ancient Egypt, the Nile flooded the land around it.

Today, many people visit Egypt to see the great pyramids.

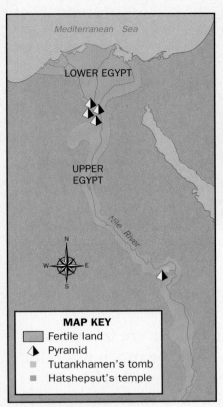

Ancient Egypt

Without the Nile River, all of the land in Egypt would be desert.

The floods left **fertile soil** on the land near the river. This soil was good for growing food. The farmers planted after the floods. If there was a lot of water in a flood, they could plant many crops. If there was not very much water, they planted fewer crops.

About 5,000 years ago, farmers found a way to use the Nile River to **irrigate** their land. They brought water from the river to use on dry land in order to grow plants and food. The farms were better and larger when people irrigated. Farmers did not have to wait until after the floods to plant their seeds. The farmers learned to work together to bring water from the Nile to their farms. People made rules as they worked together. They began to live in villages.

Soon there were many villages. Around 3100 B.C., one king began to rule all the villages in Egypt. Later, Egyptian rulers were called **pharaohs**. The pharaohs made laws for all the people of Egypt. People believed a pharaoh was both a **god** and a ruler. The pharaohs were very powerful. All farmers had to give some of their food to the pharaohs.

Most of the pharaohs were men, but one of the greatest pharaohs was a woman. Her name was Hatshepsut. Hatshepsut helped Egypt become a very rich country. She sent ships to trade items with other

Egyptian pharaoh

We have learned much about ancient Egypt from items found in Tutankhamen's tomb. This item shows the pharaoh and his wife.

King Tutankhamen

countries. Many large buildings were built when Hatshepsut was pharaoh.

Since Egypt has little rain, there are few trees. The ancient Egyptians did not have much wood for building. Instead, they often used mud bricks. The Egyptians also cut stone blocks to make buildings. Strong metal tools helped the Egyptians cut stone.

The people of ancient Egypt built large stone buildings called **pyramids** in the desert. These pyramids were built for pharaohs. Inside the pyramids were **tombs** for the dead. One of the most famous tombs was built for the young King Tutankhamen. His tomb was not in a pyramid. It was cut deep into rock.

Why did the Egyptians work so hard at building these tombs and pyramids? They built them because they believed that people lived again after they died. They believed that the dead needed a good place to spend their next lives. Egyptians put the bodies of the dead inside tombs. They left food, water, and clothing in the tomb for the dead person to use in the next life. They painted pictures of people on the walls of the tombs. The Egyptians believed that the people in these pictures would be friends with the dead person in the next life.

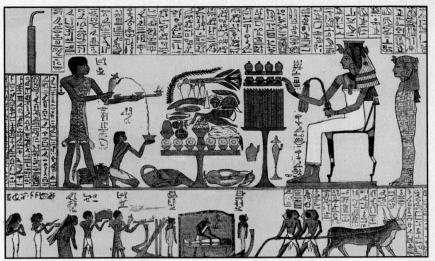
This drawing is about the death of an Egyptian queen. The many symbols in the drawing are Egyptian writing.

Archaeologists have learned about life in ancient Egypt from the paintings, foods, and other items found inside tombs and pyramids. Today there are 35 major pyramids still standing in Egypt. The oldest pyramids are almost 5,000 years old.

Many people in Egypt were **slaves**. Slaves were not free men and women. They were not paid for their work. Slaves were forced to build pyramids for the pharaohs. Thousands of slaves built the pyramids. They built many other buildings, too.

The Egyptians were some of the first people to write their words. At first they used tiny pictures to show the words. They needed many small pictures. Then they wrote small signs to show different sounds and ideas. Egyptian writing had more than 800 signs. Archaeologists have found papers and stones with Egyptian writing. We have learned much about the ancient Egyptians by reading their writing.

Ancient Egypt was a great country for more than 2,800 years. As time passed, the pharaohs had less power. Other people gained control of the land, and the pharaohs lost their power. Egypt became weak. Then other countries ruled Egypt.

In the next chapter, you will read about other great people of long ago.

Cup from King Tutankhamen's tomb

Hatshepsut

Hatshepsut was one of the few women to rule ancient Egypt. Many people believe she was one of the greatest pharaohs. Hatshepsut ruled Egypt for 21 years from about 1503 B.C. to about 1482 B.C.

Although it was a custom that pharaohs be male, Hatshepsut declared herself pharaoh. She sometimes even wore clothing that was like the clothing that male pharaohs had worn. Sometimes she also wore a false beard that was like the beards that male pharaohs had worn.

Hatshepsut brought peace to Egypt. She was one of the few pharaohs who was not interested in war. She is best known for her interests in trading and building.

During Hatshepsut's rule, Egyptian traders went on ships to other lands in eastern Africa. The Egyptian traders took their beads, metal tools, and **weapons** to trade. In exchange the traders received such things as ivory, gold, live animals, and trees. Egypt became very rich because of this trade.

Many buildings were made during Hatshepsut's rule. One huge **temple** was built for Hatshepsut. This famous temple was built into the sides of hills. Hatshepsut planned that this temple would be her tomb when she died. She had the walls of the temple decorated with pictures. The pictures tell the story of the important events during Hatshepsut's rule. One story tells about the Egyptian trade in eastern Africa.

Hatshepsut's temple is still standing. It is considered one of the greatest buildings in Egypt. Each year many people visit the temple. There they learn about the history of ancient Egypt during this great pharaoh's rule.

Queen Hatshepsut

Hatshepsut's temple

Questions about People in History are shown with this star on the Using What You Learned pages.

14

Using Vocabulary

Match Up   Finish the sentences in Group A with words from Group B.
Write the letter of each correct answer on the blank line.

Group A

1. The _____ from the Nile floods
was good for growing crops.

2. To _____ their land, farmers
brought water from the Nile River.

3. Hatshepsut had people build a
_____ as a place for the gods.

4. Some tombs were inside large,
stone buildings called _____ .

Group B

a. pyramids

b. temple

c. irrigate

d. fertile soil

Skill Builder

Understanding A.D. and B.C. on a Time Line   Dates tell us when events
in history happened. We say that events happened before or after the birth
of a man called Jesus. A **time line** helps us show which events happened
first. Look at the time line below. Events that happened before Jesus' birth
are marked **B.C.** Events that happened after Jesus' birth are marked **A.D.** When
counting B.C. years, the highest number tells the oldest event. When counting
A.D. years, the lowest number tells the oldest event.

0 Jesus is born.

3100 B.C. Ancient
Egypt begins.

1503 B.C. Hatshepsut
becomes pharaoh.

A.D. 476 The Roman
Empire ends.

| B.C. | 3500 | 3000 | 2500 | 2000 | 1500 | 1000 | 500 | 0 | 500 | 1000 | A.D. |

Circle the older date in each pair.

1. 1503 B.C.   3100 B.C.

2. 3100 B.C.   A.D. 476

3. A.D. 1503   1503 B.C.

4. A.D. 476   0

Read and Remember

Finish Up   Choose a word in dark print to best complete each sentence. Write the word on the correct blank line.

Hatshepsut   civilization   Nile   Egyptians   slaves

1. Ancient Egypt has been called the "gift of the _____."

2. The pharaoh was the ruler of all _____.

3. _____ was known for her interests in building and trading.

4. The _____ of ancient Egypt lasted for more than 2,800 years.

5. Egyptian _____ were forced to work hard without pay.

Think and Apply

Cause and Effect   A **cause** is something that makes something else happen. What happens is called the **effect**.

> **Cause** Stone Age people learned to farm.
> **Effect** People did not need to move from place to place to find food.

Match each cause on the left with an effect on the right. Write the letter of the effect on the correct blank. The first one is done for you.

Cause

1. Ancient Egyptians believed in life after death, so __d__

2. Farmers in ancient Egypt found a way to irrigate dry land, so _____

3. Ancient Egypt had few trees, so _____

4. Archaeologists have learned to read stones with Egyptian writing, so _____

Effect

a. they have learned a lot about the ancient Egyptians.

b. they did not have to wait until after the floods to plant their seeds.

c. many buildings were made from stone blocks.

d. they left food and clothing in tombs.

People of the Fertile Crescent

THINK ABOUT AS YOU READ

1. Why did many people want to live near the Fertile Crescent?
2. Why were Sumerian priests such a powerful group?
3. Why was Hammurabi a great king for Babylonia?

NEW WORDS

♦ crescent
♦ scarce
♦ city-states
♦ priests
♦ classes
♦ conquered

PEOPLE & PLACES

♦ Middle East
♦ Tigris River
♦ Euphrates River
♦ Fertile Crescent
♦ Mesopotamia
♦ Sumerians
♦ Babylonians
♦ Hammurabi
♦ Babylonian Empire

Egypt and the Nile River are in an area that today we call the Middle East. Two other long rivers in the Middle East are the Tigris River and the Euphrates River. Like the Nile River, the two rivers sometimes flooded the land around them. The floods brought fertile soil to the land. The land around the rivers and to the west forms a **crescent** shape. This area is called the Fertile Crescent. The land between the two rivers was once called Mesopotamia. Thousands of years ago, civilizations developed in Mesopotamia and the Fertile Crescent.

Most of the Middle East is hot, dry land with little rain. Water is **scarce** in most of the Middle East. Many people in this area wanted to live near the rivers and the good soil of the Fertile Crescent.

The Sumerians were the first people we know of who lived in Mesopotamia. They lived there from about 3500 B.C. to about 2000 B.C. They became good

The Sumerians were some of the first people to use wheels.

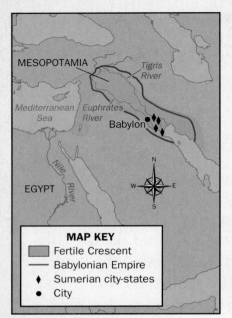
Fertile Crescent

Sumerian temple

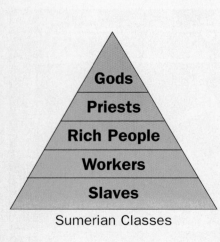
Sumerian Classes

farmers at about the same time as the Egyptians. The Sumerians worked together to irrigate their farms. Sometimes floods would destroy good crops. The Sumerians learned to control the floods. They built strong walls near the rivers. The walls stopped the river water from covering the land.

The Sumerians created a system to write their words and numbers. Their writing was made of many small signs. They wrote on pieces of wet clay. They dried the clay in the sun.

The Sumerians built many **city-states** where people lived and worked together. Each city-state had its own ruler. The city-states fought with each other to win control of all of Mesopotamia.

The Sumerians believed that many gods ruled the earth. The gods let people grow food. In return the people had to work for their gods. They gave the gods food and clothing. **Priests** worked in temples for the gods. The Sumerians believed that only priests knew what the gods wanted. The people had to obey the priests in order to please the gods. This made the priests very powerful.

The Sumerians divided people into different groups called **classes**. Every Sumerian belonged to a class. Priests were the most powerful class. Rich people were also a powerful class. Workers were in another class. Slaves were in the lowest class. Many people were slaves.

Around 1800 B.C. people from another part of Mesopotamia **conquered** the Sumerians. These people were the Babylonians. The Babylonians learned much from the Sumerians. They learned to write on wet clay. They learned to be good farmers.

The Babylonians had a great king. His name was Hammurabi. He ruled from about 1792 B.C. to 1750 B.C. During that time he conquered most of the Fertile Crescent. The land he conquered became part of the Babylonian Empire, or Babylonia. The people

One Babylonian king had people build the Hanging Gardens of Babylon for his wife.

Sumerian clay tablet with writing

Hammurabi talking to a god

of Babylonia traded with people in Egypt and with people in other far-off lands.

Hammurabi became famous because he put all of the laws of his empire together. He put together almost 300 laws. These laws were written on a very large stone. The stone was placed where all the people could read it. The laws were called the Code of Hammurabi.

What kind of laws were on the stone? Some laws said that strong people should not hurt weak people. One law said that if a man destroyed the eye of another person, that man's own eye must be destroyed. Many laws had to do with land, money, and family life. Some laws were fair to women. Women could own land. The Code of Hammurabi was written for all Babylonians.

The Babylonian Empire grew weaker after Hammurabi died. Many people wanted to rule the fertile land around the rivers. There were many wars. The Fertile Crescent was conquered again and again.

In the next chapter, you will read about other people who lived in the Middle East long ago.

Using Vocabulary

Finish Up   Choose a word in dark print to best complete each sentence. Write the word on the correct blank line.

crescent   priests   conquered   scarce   city-states

1. There was little rain in the Middle East, so water was _____.

2. The fertile area around the Tigris and Euphrates rivers has a long, curved _____ shape.

3. The Sumerians built many _____ where people lived and worked together.

4. The _____ were the most powerful Sumerian class because they worked for the gods.

5. The Babylonians became the rulers of the Sumerians when they fought and _____ the Sumerians.

Read and Remember

Find the Answer   Put a check (✔) next to each sentence that tells something true about the Fertile Crescent and its peoples. You should check four sentences.

_____ **1.** The Fertile Crescent is the land around the Nile River.

_____ **2.** Many people wanted to control the land of the Fertile Crescent.

_____ **3.** The Sumerians built only one city-state.

_____ **4.** The Sumerians believed that many gods ruled the earth.

_____ **5.** The Sumerians were divided into classes.

_____ **6.** Hammurabi put together laws for his empire.

_____ **7.** The Babylonians wrote on paper instead of clay or stone.

Think and Apply

Compare and Contrast   Read each sentence below. Decide whether it tells about Sumerians, Babylonians, or both groups of people. Write **S** next to each sentence that tells about Sumerians. Write **B** next to each sentence that tells about Babylonians. Write **SB** next to each sentence that tells about both Sumerians and Babylonians. The first one is done for you.

SB   **1.** The people lived in the Fertile Crescent.

_____   **2.** The people lived in city-states.

_____   **3.** The people were the first people we know of in Mesopotamia.

_____   **4.** The people were part of an empire.

_____   **5.** The people had to follow Hammurabi's laws.

_____   **6.** The people could write their own words.

_____   **7.** Around 1800 B.C. these people were conquered by people from another part of Mesopotamia.

_____   **8.** The people were good farmers.

Skill Builder

Using Map Keys   Sometimes a map uses a color or a symbol to show something on the map. A **map key** tells what the color or the symbol means. Look at the map of the Fertile Crescent on page 18. Study the map and the map key. Then write the answer to each question below.

1. What is the symbol for a Sumerian city-state?_____

2. What is the symbol for a city?_____

3. What color is used to show the Fertile Crescent?_____

4. Was Babylon a city or a city-state?_____

5. Was the Nile River part of the Babylonian Empire?_____

CHAPTER 4

Other People of the Ancient Middle East

In this chapter you will read about other people who lived in the Middle East. Two of these groups, the Phoenicians and the Jews, lived near the Mediterranean Sea. Another group, the Persians, conquered most of the Middle East.

Early Phoenicians lived near the Mediterranean Sea at about the same time that the Sumerians lived in the Fertile Crescent. The Phoenicians, however, became a great sea power by the year 1000 B.C. The map on page 23 shows where the Phoenicians lived. The Phoenicians built good ships. They sailed in their ships to many far-off places. They traded in other lands. They brought back many items from their trips.

The Phoenicians were the first people to use an **alphabet** for writing. They made an alphabet with 22 letters. The Phoenician alphabet was simpler than Egyptian signs or Sumerian signs. The ancient

The Phoenicians sailed to many far-off places.

Phoenician About 1000 B.C.	Modern
⪦	A
⪄	B
⪁	C
◁	D
Y	F,U,V,W,Y
⪥	H
∟	L
ⱳ	M
O	O
φ	Q
+	T

Some letters of the Phoenician alphabet

Phoenicia and Palestine

Jerusalem is a city with many ancient buildings and modern buildings.

Egyptians and other people of the Middle East had to know hundreds of signs in order to write. The Phoenicians only had to know 22 letters! The alphabet we use today comes from the Phoenician alphabet of long ago.

The Jews were another group of people who lived near the Mediterranean Sea. The Jews lived in a land that became known as Palestine. Today part of the land of Palestine is called Israel. The capital city is Jerusalem.

The Jews had their own **religion**. It was called **Judaism**. People who believe in Judaism believe in only one god. The Jews were the first people that we know of to believe in one god. Other people of the Middle East believed in many gods.

For a long time, there was not very much food to eat in Palestine. There was a lot of food in Egypt. The Egyptians had food in difficult times because they had saved food in large buildings. They saved this food for the times when farmers would not be able to grow enough food. So the Jews left Palestine and went to live in Egypt. As time passed, there were many Jews in Egypt.

Moses led the Jews out of Egypt.

Moses with the Ten Commandments

The Egyptian pharaoh made the Jews work as slaves. The Jews were forced to build tombs and pyramids. Jews who did not want to work as slaves were beaten or killed.

Around 1200 B.C., a man named Moses became the leader of the Jews in Egypt. Moses and the Jews left Egypt. They went into the desert between Egypt and Palestine. They were in the desert for forty years.

In the desert Moses showed the Jews two large stones. Ten laws were written on the stones. These laws were called the **Ten Commandments**. Jews believe that God gave these laws to Moses in the desert. The laws teach people to be kind, fair, and **honest**. One law says that people must not steal. Another law says that people must not kill or hurt other people. Today these laws are an important part

Jews praying in Jerusalem

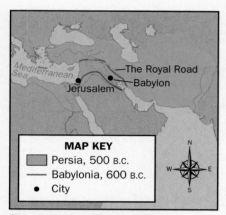
The Persian Empire, 500 B.C.

Persian coin

of Judaism. The laws later became part of another religion called **Christianity**. You will learn more about Christianity in Chapter 10.

The Jews wrote down their history in a book. This book became the first part of the **Bible**. The stories about the Jews of long ago and the laws of Moses are in the **Old Testament** of the Bible. People have been reading the Bible for many years.

After the Jews were in the desert for forty years, they went back to Palestine. The Jews conquered Palestine. Many years later the Jews were also conquered. They were conquered by the new rulers of the Fertile Crescent. Then in 586 B.C., Palestine was conquered again. This time the Jews were conquered by the Babylonians. The Jews were forced to leave Palestine. Many Jews were taken to Babylon to live. They did not want to live in Babylon. But they continued to believe in Judaism while they were in Babylon.

About 539 B.C. the Persians took control of Babylonia. The Persians conquered most of the Middle East. They even conquered part of Europe. No other people of the ancient world conquered as much land as did the Persians.

One Persian king said the Jews could go back to Palestine. Thousands of Jews left Babylon. They made Palestine their home again.

The Persians were good rulers. They were fair to the people they conquered. They built many good roads in the countries they ruled. The Persians had a good way to send letters. People on horses carried letters all over the empire. The Persians also used metal coins as a system of money.

The Persians ruled the Middle East for more than 200 years. Then they, too, were conquered. Who conquered the Persians? You will learn the answer to that question in Chapter 7.

Using Vocabulary

Find the Meaning   Write on the blank the word or words that best complete each sentence.

1. A **religion** is a belief in _____ .

   a pharaoh   one god or many gods   a ruler

2. An **alphabet** has _____ that people use in their writing.

   pencils   clay   letters

3. **Judaism** and **Christianity** are religions that share _____ .

   money and rulers   laws and ideas   buildings and farms

4. The **Ten Commandments** are laws that Jews believe _____ gave to Moses in the desert.

   God   the Phoenicians   Tutankhamen

5. The **Old Testament** of the Bible tells the history of the _____ of long ago.

   Persians   Phoenicians   Jews

Read and Remember

Choose the Answer   Draw a circle around the correct answer.

1. Where did the Phoenicians and the Jews live?

   near the Mediterranean Sea   near the Tigris River   near the Pacific Ocean

2. Where did the Jews first live?

   Persia   Egypt   Palestine

3. Who conquered Babylonia?

   Egyptians   Persians   Phoenicians

4. What did the Persians build in the countries they ruled?

   good roads   pyramids   tombs

Finish Up   Choose a word in dark print to best complete each sentence. Write the word on the correct blank line.

food   ships   Palestine   Babylon   honest   Phoenician

1. The Phoenicians built many good _____.

2. The alphabet we use today comes from the _____ alphabet.

3. The Jews went to Egypt because they needed _____.

4. The Ten Commandments teach people to be kind and _____.

5. The Jews conquered _____ after living in the desert for forty years.

6. A Persian king said that the Jews could leave _____.

Journal Writing

Write a short paragraph about the Phoenician alphabet. Tell why it was easier to use than Egyptian or Sumerian writing.

Think and Apply

Categories   Read the words in each group. Decide how they are alike. Find the best title for each group from the words in dark print. Write the title on the line above each group. The first one is done for you.

Persians   Phoenicians   Judaism   Moses

1. _____Phoenicians_____
built ships
good traders
made writing easier

2. _____
led Jews from Egypt
Ten Commandments
1200 B.C.

3. _____
one god
Old Testament
Jews

4. _____
conquered Babylonia
good rulers
metal coins

Skill Builder

Reading a Chart   A **chart** lists a group of facts. Charts help you learn facts quickly. Read the chart below about groups of people who lived in the ancient Middle East. Then write the answer to each question.

PEOPLE IN THE ANCIENT MIDDLE EAST

People	Kinds of Rulers	Types of Work	Interesting Facts
Egyptians	pharaohs	farming, raising animals, trading	Built tombs for dead people. Egypt's doctors were well known for their medical services.
Sumerians	priests and kings	farming, raising animals, trading	Believed all parts of nature, such as wind, rain, and floods, were gods. Created a system of writing.
Babylonians	kings	farming, raising animals, trading	Believed in many gods. Created an important set of laws.
Phoenicians	kings and rich traders	sailing, exploring new lands, trading	Explored the Mediterranean Sea. Made an expensive purple dye that was usually sold to kings and their families.
Jews	judges at first; later ruled by kings	farming, raising animals, trading	Had laws called the Ten Commandments. Believed in one god.
Persians	kings; other leaders for smaller parts of the empire	farming, raising animals, trading	Built a road that was 1,677 miles long. Used coins for money.

1. What kinds of rulers did the Sumerians have?_____

2. Which group of people was first ruled by judges?_____

3. Which group of people sailed, explored new lands, and traded?_____

4. How many of the groups shown on the chart farmed, raised animals,

and traded?_____

5. Based on the chart, what is one interesting fact about Egyptians?_____

_____

6. Which group of people built a long road?_____

Life in Ancient India

We use numbers every day. Numbers are on money and on pages of books. Long ago the people of ancient India began to use numbers. We use the same kind of numbers today that the ancient Indians used. Our numbers are more than 1,500 years old.

India is a large country in southern Asia. India is separated from the rest of Asia by the Himalayas. The Himalayas are very tall mountains.

The Indus River was an important river in ancient India. The land around the river has very fertile soil. Today the land around the Indus River is part of the country called Pakistan. Pakistan was once part of India.

Civilizations in ancient India began near the Indus River. They began around the year 2500 B.C. Do you remember how the Egyptians and the Sumerians used water and fertile soil from their rivers to grow

The ancient city of Mohenjo-Daro was built near the Indus River.

The Aryans made Hinduism an important religion. Here a Hindu god is holding up a mountain.

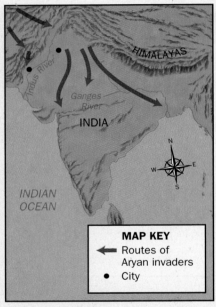
Ancient India

MAP KEY
← Routes of Aryan invaders
• City

food? The ancient Indian farmers also did this. They used water from the Indus River for **irrigation**.

The ancient Indians built cities near the Indus River. These were large cities with straight streets and brick houses. The ancient Indians made metal tools. They created a writing system. They did not have an alphabet. Their writing was made of many tiny pictures and numbers.

About 1500 B.C. people from a far-off land conquered the land around the Indus River. These people were called Aryans. We are not sure from where the Aryans came. Many people believe that Aryans may have come from the Middle East.

The Aryans were good fighters. They conquered all of the land around the Indus River. They conquered much of India. The Aryans became farmers. They also raised cows and sheep. They made many Indians work as their slaves.

The Aryans changed India in many ways. These changes are an important part of Indian life today. One change was that family life in India became very

Farmers in India were in the third caste.

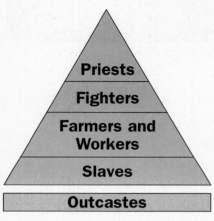

Priests

Fighters

Farmers and Workers

Slaves

Outcastes

Castes in Ancient India

A Hindu god

important. Another change was that a family's wealth was based on the number of cows the family had. A third change was that the Aryans made **Hinduism,** or the Hindu religion, important. Millions of Indians believe in Hinduism today. These people are called Hindus. Hinduism is the main religion in India today. A fourth change was the growth of the **caste system**.

Under the caste system, all people belonged to different groups. These groups became known as **castes**. Castes became part of the Hindu religion. There were four main castes. The priests and their families were in the highest caste. Priests worked in the temples for the gods. Rulers and fighters were in the next caste. Farmers and workers were in the third caste. Servants and slaves were in the lowest caste. A large group of people were not in any caste at all. These people were called **outcastes**. Indians in the four castes tried to stay away from the outcastes. The outcastes were forced to do the worst jobs.

People were born into the caste of their parents. People could not change castes. A farmer could not become a priest. People could only marry those from their own caste.

The Aryans believed that all people were **reborn** after they died. They believed that good people were reborn into a better caste. A good person might be reborn as a priest. A bad person might be reborn as a slave or an outcaste. The Aryans also believed there were many gods. These ideas became part of the Hindu religion.

Buddhism, or the Buddhist religion, also began in ancient India. It began about the year 500 B.C. Buddhism began with a man in India who became known as the Buddha. The Buddha did not believe in the Hindu gods. The Buddha taught that people should not be put into castes. He taught that people must be good and kind to each other. The Buddha said that people would be happy when they did not care about owning money, jewelry, or other items.

These Hindus are praying along the Ganges River in India.

Buddha statue

Many Indians liked what the Buddha said. People who believed in what the Buddha said were called Buddhists. This religion was spread from India to most of Asia by Buddhist **monks**. They started Buddhist schools in many parts of Asia. Buddhism became one of the major religions of the world. However, more Indians today follow Hinduism than follow Buddhism.

The Aryans ruled much of northern India for about 1,000 years. Then the Persians from the Middle East conquered the Aryans. The Persians ruled northern India for about 200 years. They, too, were conquered by other people. India was conquered many times during its long history.

The ancient Indians gave the world many important ideas. Hinduism and Buddhism came from India. Our numbers were first made by the people of ancient India. Ancient Indians were also known for their work in science.

Another ancient group of people lived in Asia. Like the ancient Indians, these people also had many important ideas that we still use today. You will read about these people in the next chapter.

Using Vocabulary

Finish the Paragraph   Use the words in dark print to finish the paragraph below. Write on the correct blank lines the words you choose.

outcastes   **Buddhism**   **castes**   **reborn**   **Hinduism**

The Aryans made _____ an important religion. This religion divided people into four groups called _____. People who did not belong to one of the four groups were _____. The Aryans believed that after people died they were _____ as another living thing. About 500 B.C. in India, the Buddha started a new religion called _____. This religion said that people would be happy when they did not care about owning things.

Read and Remember

Finish the Sentence   Draw a circle around the word or words that best complete each sentence.

1. The ancient Indians used water from the _____ for irrigation.
Mediterranean Sea   Nile River   Indus River

2. The _____ we use today were created by the ancient Indians.
numbers   ships   alphabets

3. The _____ made family life in India important.
Egyptians   Aryans   Persians

4. The _____ did not believe in the Hindu gods.
Aryans   Buddha   Indians

5. _____ believed that people should not be divided into groups.
Aryans   Buddhists   Hindus

Think and Apply

Distinguishing Relevant Information   Information that is **relevant** is information that is important for what you want to say or write. Imagine that you want to tell a friend about life in ancient India. Then read each sentence below. Decide which sentences are relevant to what you will say. Put a check (✔) next to the relevant sentences. There are four relevant sentences. The first one is done for you.

_✔_ **1.** Farmers irrigated fertile soil near the river in order to grow crops.

_____ **2.** People in ancient India built brick houses and large cities.

_____ **3.** A family's wealth was based on the number of cows the family had.

_____ **4.** The Himalayas are very tall mountains.

_____ **5.** Hinduism is the main religion in India today.

_____ **6.** Many Indians believed in what the Buddha said.

_____ **7.** Pakistan was once part of India.

Skill Builder

Reading a Diagram   A **diagram** is a way of showing information. Study the diagram of the Indian caste system on page 31. Then write the answer to each question.

1. Who belonged to the highest caste? _____

2. Who belonged to the lowest caste? _____

3. Which castes were higher than the caste of farmers and workers? _____

_____

4. Which group was not in a caste? _____

Journal Writing

Write a paragraph about the ways the Aryans changed India.

Life in Ancient China

THINK ABOUT AS YOU READ

1. How was ancient China ruled?
2. What was the Great Wall of China?
3. What kinds of things did the ancient Chinese know how to make?

NEW WORDS

- dynasties
- invaded
- soldiers
- respected
- silk
- china
- civil service system

PEOPLE & PLACES

- China
- Huang He
- Chinese
- Beijing
- Han Dynasty
- Great Wall of China
- Confucius

China is a very large country in eastern Asia. The ancient civilization of China began around 3000 B.C. It began near a very long river called the Huang He. *Huang He* means "Yellow River."

Chinese people farmed the fertile soil along the Huang He. They used the Huang He to irrigate their farms. The Huang He often flooded the land. The floods sometimes destroyed farms, houses, and even whole villages. When this happened, the people called the river "China's Sorrow." The Chinese began to work together to stop the floods. They built strong dirt walls near the river. Sometimes these walls stopped the floods from destroying their farms.

China was ruled by **dynasties** for thousands of years. A dynasty is a family of kings. When the ruling king died, his oldest son became the new king. When that king died, his oldest son became the next king.

Many people visit the Great Wall in China each year.

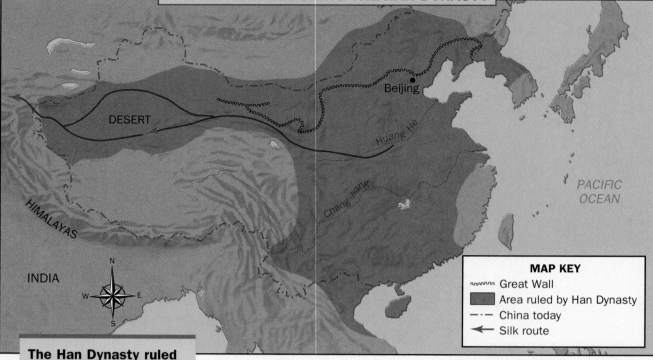

DESERT

Beijing

Huang He

HIMALAYAS

INDIA

Chang Jiang

PACIFIC OCEAN

N
W E
S

MAP KEY
〜〜〜 Great Wall
▨ Area ruled by Han Dynasty
—·— China today
◄— Silk route

The Han Dynasty ruled much land in ancient China. Is China today larger or smaller than the land that the Han Dynasty ruled?

Huang He

The first dynasty began its rule around 1700 B.C. Some dynasties ruled China for hundreds of years. Many dynasties ruled from the city of Beijing.

The Han Dynasty was one of the greatest dynasties. The Han family became rulers in 202 B.C. They ruled ancient China for more than 400 years. China became strong and rich during the Han Dynasty. The Han Dynasty conquered much of Asia. During this time China began to trade with people to the west. They even traded with people as far away as Europe.

Sometimes people from the north **invaded** China. In 221 B.C. the Chinese began building a tall, strong wall. The Great Wall of China was about 1,500 miles long. It was about 20 feet high and very wide. It took many years to build the wall. The wall helped keep out people that were invading from the north. **Soldiers** stood on top of the Great Wall to watch for invading people. The wall helped keep the Chinese people safe. Many years later the Chinese made the wall much longer. The Great Wall is still standing in China today.

Families in China often worked together.

Chinese writing with drawings of Buddha

Confucius teaching his ideas

Many people in ancient China followed the ideas of Buddha. The Chinese also followed the ideas of another great teacher. His name was Confucius. Confucius lived about 2,500 years ago. He taught many important ideas about people, government, and family.

Confucius believed that people should be helpful, kind, and honest. He told people to obey their rulers. He said that rulers must be fair to their people. Confucius also taught that the family was the most important group in Chinese life. He said that family members should take care of one another. He taught that older members of the family should always be **respected**.

Family life was very important in ancient China. Children obeyed their parents. After a man and a women were married, they lived in the house of the husband's parents. As the family grew bigger, they built new rooms onto the house. In some families one hundred people lived in one home. The large families worked together on farms. Family life is still very important in China today.

For hundreds of years, the Chinese would not share their secrets of making silk.

Vase made of china

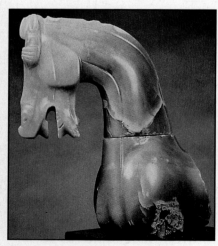
Art from the Han Dynasty

The Chinese created their own system of writing. Their writing had thousands of signs. The Chinese had a sign for every word. A Chinese person had to learn thousands of signs in order to read and write. Chinese writing today still has thousands of signs.

The Chinese knew how to make many things. They could make strong metal tools. They made carts that had wheels. These carts were pulled by horses. Almost 5,000 years ago, Chinese people began to make beautiful soft cloth called **silk**. For hundreds of years, the Chinese would not tell anyone how to make silk cloth. China made a lot of money by selling silk to other countries. Chinese people traveled on a long road to trade their silk in lands west of China. Around A.D. 600 the Chinese began to make thin, delicate dishes out of white clay. Today these fine dishes are called **china**.

The Chinese were the first people to make paper as we know it today. They made paper from rags. Then the Chinese learned how to print paper books. People in Europe did not begin printing paper books until hundreds of years later.

The ancient Chinese found ways to do many things that people in other areas of the world did not yet know how to do. Today we still use many of the ideas we learned from the ancient Chinese.

Confucius (551–479 B.C.)

Confucius was teaching in China at about the same time that people in India were learning from the Buddha. Confucius taught all students that wanted to learn. He gave people rules about how to behave. He taught that people should treat others the same way they would want to be treated. Confucius said, "What you do not want done to you, do not do to others."

Confucius lived during a time of much war in China. Rulers in different parts of China often fought with each other. Confucius believed that there could only be peace if there was a good government. He believed that a ruler should be good and honest to the people. Then the people would obey the ruler.

Confucius

Confucius wanted an important position in the government. Then he could teach his ideas to kings and to many more people. But he never got the job he wanted. After Confucius died, some of his students continued to teach his sayings to other people. They also wrote his ideas and sayings in books.

More than 300 years after Confucius died, rulers in the Han Dynasty began to study his ideas. Confucius had believed that government workers should earn their jobs by doing good work. This is why the Han Dynasty set up a **civil service system**. Through the civil service system, people could get government jobs. To get a government job, a person had to first pass a civil service test about the ideas of Confucius.

Confucius was a great thinker and a wise teacher. His ideas about government and how to behave are studied all over the world today.

Questions about People in History are shown with this star on the Using What You Learned pages.

Using Vocabulary

Match Up   Finish the sentences in Group A with words from Group B.
Write the letter of each correct answer on the blank line.

Group A

1. Families of kings called _____ ruled China for thousands of years.

2. China was attacked when people from the north _____ the country.

3. One way a person might show _____ for the older members of a family is to listen to their ideas.

4. A test for a government job in China was a _____ test.

5. The Chinese _____ were people whose main job was to protect China.

Group B

a. invaded

b. soldiers

c. civil service

d. respect

e. dynasties

Read and Remember

Finish the Paragraph   Use the words in dark print to finish the paragraph
below. Write on the correct blank lines the words you choose.

china   silk   Huang He   Great Wall

The people of ancient China knew how to make many things. They built

dirt walls to stop the floods of the _____ from destroying their

farms. To help keep China safe, they built the _____ . The people

of ancient China made beautiful _____ cloth. They also used

white clay to make dishes called _____ . The Chinese also knew

how to make paper and strong metal tools.

Write the Answer   Write one or more sentences to answer each question.

1. What are two changes that occurred during the Han Dynasty?_____

_____

2. What was family life like in ancient China?_____

_____

⭐ **3.** Why did Confucius want an important position in the government?_____

_____

⭐ **4.** Why did the Han Dynasty set up the civil service system?_____

_____

Journal Writing

Write a few sentences about some of the important ideas of Confucius.

Think and Apply

Fact or Opinion   A **fact** is a true statement. An **opinion** is a statement that tells what a person thinks.

> **Fact** The Han Dynasty ruled ancient China for more than 400 years.
> **Opinion** The Han Dynasty was the greatest dynasty in the history of China.

Write **F** next to each fact below. Write **O** next to each opinion. You should find two sentences that are opinions.

_____ **1.** The Great Wall was about 1,500 miles long.

_____ **2.** People should study the ideas of Confucius.

_____ **3.** Ancient Chinese writing had thousands of signs.

_____ **4.** Buddha was a better teacher than Confucius was.

_____ **5.** Many dynasties ruled from the city of Beijing.

Unit 2 Two Thousand Years of Change

From 800 B.C. to A.D. 1500, the world changed in many ways. New empires began. People fought wars about lands, religions, and ideas. People learned new ways to make books and art. Populations increased. Trade also increased. People traded spices and crops. They also traded ideas. New ideas about government would be followed for hundreds of years to come.

Who were some of the people of those times? The ancient Greeks gave the world the first ideas about government run by the people. The ancient Romans gave the world new ideas about laws. People in the Byzantine Empire enjoyed new ideas about art, science, building, and learning. Muslims and Christians spread their religions to many lands. During those years people fought many wars. They killed one another and destroyed towns and farms. Sometimes wars helped people learn about new ideas. Some wars also helped to increase trade. Wars changed the way people lived.

What happened to the people of ancient Greece and Rome? How did two religions change the way many people lived? What changes happened during the long years of the Middle Ages? As you read Unit Two, think

about some of the changes that happened between 800 B.C. and A.D. 1500. Think about how the ideas from that time period affect our lives today.

753 B.C. Ancient Rome begins.	**508 B.C.** Athens becomes a democracy.		**476** Rome falls.	**1071** The Turks capture Jerusalem.
	323 B.C. Alexander the Great dies.	**49 B.C.** Julius Caesar becomes the Roman leader.	**622** Muhammad flees to Mecca.	**1295** Marco Polo returns to Italy from China.
		0 Jesus Christ is born.		

B.C. | 800 | 400 | 0 | 400 | 800 | 1200 | 1600 | A.D.

27 B.C.–A.D. 476 Roman Empire

A.D. 476–A.D. 1500 Middle Ages

700–1400 Feudalism in Europe

1095–1291 Crusades

CHAPTER 7

The Story of Ancient Greece

THINK ABOUT AS YOU READ

1. **How were the Greek city-states of Athens and Sparta different?**
2. **How was Athens a democracy?**
3. **What did the people of ancient Greece give the world?**

NEW WORDS

- ◆ **peninsula**
- ◆ **colonies**
- ◆ **citizens**
- ◆ **democracy**
- ◆ **culture**
- ◆ **Golden Age**

PEOPLE & PLACES

- ◆ **Greece**
- ◆ **Greeks**
- ◆ **Black Sea**
- ◆ **Sparta**
- ◆ **Athens**
- ◆ **Aspasia**
- ◆ **Socrates**
- ◆ **Aristotle**
- ◆ **Philip II**
- ◆ **Alexander the Great**
- ◆ **Pericles**
- ◆ **Parthenon**

Greece is a small country in Europe. It is near the Mediterranean Sea. The main part of Greece is on a **peninsula**. A peninsula is a body of land with water on almost all sides. The rest of Greece is made up of islands. The ancient civilization of Greece began around 3000 B.C.

Unlike India and China, ancient Greece did not begin near a river. There are few rivers and little fertile soil in Greece. The Greeks could not grow enough food. They needed to get food from other lands.

The Mediterranean Sea was important to ancient Greece. Long ago the Greeks built ships. They sailed on the Mediterranean Sea and on the Black Sea. They sailed to many far-off places. They built Greek **colonies** in these far-off places. The Greeks brought food from their colonies back to Greece.

Greece has many tall mountains. Around 800 B.C. the Greeks began to build many city-states on the flat

The Greeks built many temples for their gods. This temple is called the Parthenon.

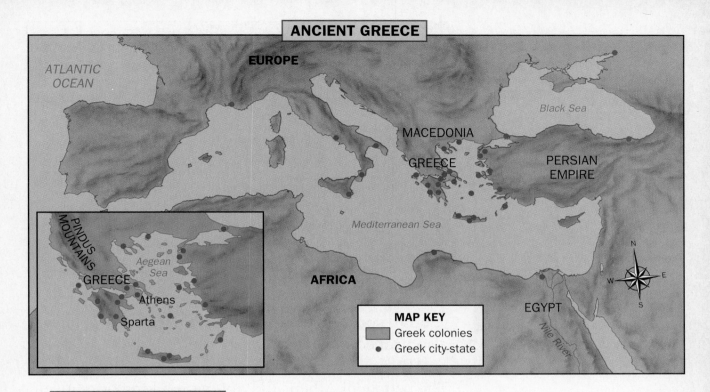

ATLANTIC OCEAN

EUROPE

Black Sea

MACEDONIA

GREECE

PERSIAN EMPIRE

PINDUS MOUNTAINS

Aegean Sea

GREECE

Athens

Sparta

Mediterranean Sea

AFRICA

EGYPT

Nile River

N
W E
S

MAP KEY
Greek colonies
• Greek city-state

The Greeks sailed to and from their colonies. Which two bodies of water did they have to cross to reach their different colonies?

Spartan soldier

land between the mountains. The mountains kept the people of Greece apart. Each city-state had its own laws, rulers, and money.

Sparta was an important city-state in Greece. It was very large and powerful. It had a well-trained army. It conquered other city-states to gain wealth and power. The government of Sparta had two kings.

Sparta had three classes. The first class was **citizens**. Not all people in Sparta were citizens. Only men born in Sparta were citizens. The women of Sparta were not citizens. However, women were allowed to own land and businesses. Women in Sparta had more freedom than women in any other city-state in Greece. The second class in Sparta was people who came from other Greek city-states or from other countries. Many of these people owned businesses. The third class was slaves.

Learning to read and to write was not very important in Sparta. Training to become good soldiers was important. Young boys were taken from their parents. They were trained to be soldiers and to be

The people of Athens started the first democracy.

Spartan woman

Greek About 600 B.C.	Modern
A	A
B	B
Γ	C
Δ	D
F	E
Ө	H
I	I,J
K	K
M	M
N	N
O	O
Σ	S
T	T
Y	U,V,W,Y
X	X
Z	Z

Letters of the Greek alphabet

good in sports such as running. Spartan girls were also trained to be good in sports.

Athens was another important Greek city-state. The people of Athens did not want a king or a queen. They believed people should rule themselves and run the government. Athens became the world's first **democracy** around 508 B.C. Other city-states became democracies. Today many countries use the Greek ideas about democracy.

Athens was a democracy because all citizens were allowed to vote. However, less than half of the people who lived in Athens were citizens. So less than half of the people in Athens could vote. Women and slaves could not vote. People who were born outside of Athens could not vote.

Learning was very important in Athens. There were many schools in Athens. Most boys went to school. Boys learned to read and write. They also learned many sports. Girls did not go to school. But one Greek woman thought girls should learn to read and write. Her name was Aspasia. Aspasia started a school for girls in Athens. Unlike girls in Sparta, girls in Athens were not allowed to play sports.

The Greeks liked the Phoenician alphabet. They changed the Phoenician alphabet a little, and it

Alexander the Great was one of Aristotle's students.

Socrates

Statue of Athena, a Greek goddess

became the Greek alphabet. They used this alphabet for all their writing.

Socrates was a great thinker and teacher in ancient Greece. He taught people to question their ideas. He taught people that there are right ways and wrong ways to behave. Aristotle was another famous Greek teacher and thinker. He started his own school in Athens. He wrote about science, art, and law. People today still study the ideas of Socrates and Aristotle.

The Greeks believed there were many gods. They built fine temples for their gods. They made many tall statues of the gods.

In Chapter 4 you learned that the Persians conquered most of the Middle East. The Persians also tried to conquer Greece. They conquered many Greek city-states. But the Persians could not conquer all of Greece. It took about twenty years for the people of Athens to win the war against Persia. After the war the Greek city-states were free again.

Philip II was a king from a country to the north of Greece. He conquered the Greek city-states in 338 B.C. His son, Alexander the Great, conquered many lands for Greece. Alexander and his soldiers conquered the Persian army. All the Persian lands became Greek lands. Alexander also became the

Alexander the Great conquered Persia and Egypt for Greece.

Alexander the Great

A Greek theater

ruler of Egypt and the Middle East. He conquered northern India. Then he started the long trip back to Greece. He died during the trip in 323 B.C. Alexander the Great was only 33 years old when he died. He had conquered many countries in less than ten years.

Alexander the Great brought Greek **culture** to the lands he ruled. New buildings in Persia were built to look like Greek buildings. People all over the empire began to use Greek money. People in Greece also began to use ideas from other countries. Alexander's empire became a mixture of many cultures.

The ancient Greeks gave the world many things. They started the world's first democracy. They were great builders. The Greeks built strong stone temples. They also built large theaters. Some of these buildings are still standing today. The Greeks also made fine paintings and statues. They wrote many plays. People around the world still enjoy watching the plays of ancient Greece.

Greece was a weak country after Alexander the Great died. The Greeks could not rule all the land that Alexander had conquered. The ancient Greeks were conquered by a stronger country. In the next chapter, you will read about the people who conquered the Greeks.

Pericles (490? B.C.–429 B.C.)

Pericles was a strong leader of democracy in Athens. He was the government leader of Athens from 460 B.C. to 429 B.C. While Pericles ruled Athens, the people of Athens enjoyed peace and good government. Athens became very powerful. This time became known as the **Golden Age** of Greece. It is considered to be the greatest time in the history of ancient Greece.

Pericles was born in Athens about 490 B.C. As a boy, Pericles studied with teachers who made him think and question his own ideas. This helped him become a good leader and a good speaker.

Pericles became the leader of Athens in 460 B.C. Much of Athens had been burned by the Persians when they had tried to conquer Greece. Pericles worked to make Athens beautiful. New temples and other buildings were built. The largest Greek temple was the Parthenon. It had beautiful statues and other works of art. Part of the Parthenon is still standing today. People from all over the world come to see it.

Pericles made the Athens navy stronger than it had been. He also made many changes in the government of Athens. He decided that people who worked for the government should be paid for their work. Another change allowed common people to work for the government.

Pericles worked to gain more lands for Athens. The people of Sparta became angry. They did not want Athens to gain too much power. So in 431 B.C., Sparta and other Greek city-states went to war against Athens. Pericles led his soldiers in this war until his death in 429 B.C.

Pericles

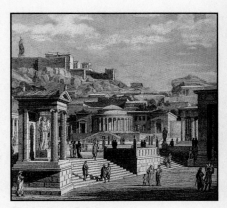

The city of Athens

Using Vocabulary

Finish Up   Choose the word or words in dark print to best complete each sentence. Write the word or words on the correct blank.

democracy   citizens   Golden Age   peninsula   colonies

1. The main part of Greece is on a _____ , or land that has water on most sides.

2. The Greek _____ were far-off places that were ruled by Greece.

3. The first class of people in Sparta were the _____ .

4. In a _____ the government is run by the people.

5. The people of Athens enjoyed peace, art, and good government during

   Greece's _____ .

Read and Remember

Who Am I?   Read each sentence. Then look at the words in dark print for the name of the person who might have said it. Write on the blank after each sentence the name of the person you choose.

Pericles   Socrates   Aristotle   Alexander the Great   Aspasia

1. "I lived in Athens where I wrote about science, art, and law."

   _____

2. "I opened a school in Athens so that girls could learn to read and write."

   _____

3. "The Parthenon was built while I was leader of Athens." _____

4. "My empire became a mixture of many cultures." _____

5. "I taught people that there are right ways and wrong ways to behave."

   _____

Journal Writing

Write a short paragraph that tells why you think Alexander became known as Alexander the Great.

Think and Apply

Understanding Different Points of View   People can look in different ways at something that happens. Look at these two points of view about Pericles.

> Pericles was the greatest leader of Athens.
> Pericles spent too many years fighting in wars.

The people of Sparta and Athens had different points of view about their ways of life. Read each sentence below. Write **Sparta** next to the sentences that might show the point of view of a person from Sparta. Write **Athens** next to the sentences that might show the point of view of a person from Athens.

_____ **1.** Women should not own land.

_____ **2.** Women should be allowed to learn sports and own land.

_____ **3.** It is better for a city-state to be ruled by kings.

_____ **4.** The people should run the government.

_____ **5.** Training to be a soldier is more important than learning to read.

_____ **6.** Boys should go to school to learn to read and write.

Sequencing Events   Write the numbers **1, 2, 3, 4,** and **5** next to these sentences to show the correct order. The first one is done for you.

_____ Philip II conquered the Greek city-states in 338 B.C.

___1___ The Greeks began to build city-states on land between the mountains.

_____ Athens and Sparta went to war in 431 B.C.

_____ Alexander the Great died in 323 B.C. after conquering many lands for Greece.

_____ Athens became a democracy around 508 B.C.

Beginning of the Roman Empire

THINK ABOUT AS YOU READ

1. **Where did the Roman Empire begin?**
2. **Why was Roman law important?**
3. **How were Julius Caesar and Augustus Caesar good rulers for Rome?**

NEW WORDS

- **conquerors**
- **republic**
- **Senate**
- **senators**
- **veto**
- **accused**
- **innocent**
- **guilty**
- **trial**
- **aqueducts**

PEOPLE & PLACES

- **Romans**
- **Italy**
- **Rome**
- **Carthage**
- **Julius Caesar**
- **Augustus Caesar**
- **Mark Antony**

The Romans were some of the greatest **conquerors** of the ancient world. The Romans built a great empire. They ruled much of the ancient world for over 900 years. The Romans thought their empire would last forever. But their empire grew weaker and weaker until it fell apart. You will read about the beginning of the Roman Empire in this chapter. In the next chapter you will read about the end of the Roman Empire.

The Roman Empire began in the country that is now called Italy. Italy is a country in Europe near the Mediterranean Sea. It is also near Greece. Like Greece, Italy is on a peninsula. Italy also has two large islands. Much of Italy has mountains.

Around 753 B.C. people began to build the city of Rome in Italy. The people of Rome were called Romans. The Romans did not want a king or a queen. Rome became a **republic**. In a republic people vote for their leaders. The Roman republic

The Romans built aqueducts to carry water into the city.

Roman women were allowed to own land and hold jobs, but they were not allowed to vote.

Roman senators

was led by the **Senate**. People in the Senate were called **senators**.

The Roman republic was not a democracy. Rich people had much more power than poor people. Poor people could not be leaders in Rome. Only some citizens were allowed to vote. Most Romans were not citizens. Most Romans could not vote. After many years some laws were changed. Poor Romans could help make laws. But the rich people of Rome still made most of the laws.

Women had more freedom in Rome than women had in Athens. They could own land and hold jobs. Women in Rome were citizens, but they were not allowed to vote.

Roman law was very important. Many Roman ideas and laws are used by countries today. The Romans used the **veto**. The veto gives government leaders the right to stop a new law from being passed. The Romans also believed that their laws should apply to all people in the empire. They believed that people **accused** of crimes were **innocent** until they were found **guilty**. Romans also believed that an accused person had a right to a fair **trial**.

The Romans borrowed many ideas from Greek culture. They believed in many of the Greek gods.

The center of the Roman Empire was the busy city of Rome.

The Roman god Neptune was also the Greek god Poseidon.

Roman soldiers

They gave these Greek gods Roman names. They made statues and pictures of their gods. They built strong temples. They built many theaters.

The Romans liked the Greek alphabet. They changed some of the Greek letters to make the Roman alphabet. Our alphabet is almost the same as the Roman alphabet.

There were many schools in the Roman Empire. Most boys and some girls went to school. They learned to read, to write, and to do math. Older children learned to read Greek in school.

The Romans built hospitals and good roads. The Romans also built bridges and **aqueducts**. Aqueducts were used to bring water to the city. Some of these roads, bridges, and aqueducts are still in use today.

The Romans had a very strong army. The Roman army conquered all of Italy. There had been Greek colonies in Italy. The Romans conquered these colonies. Later, the Romans conquered all of Greece.

The empire became even greater when the Romans conquered Carthage. Carthage was a great city in North Africa. It was near the Mediterranean Sea. The Phoenicians had built the city of Carthage. Carthage ruled many colonies near the Mediterranean Sea. Find Carthage on the map on page 55.

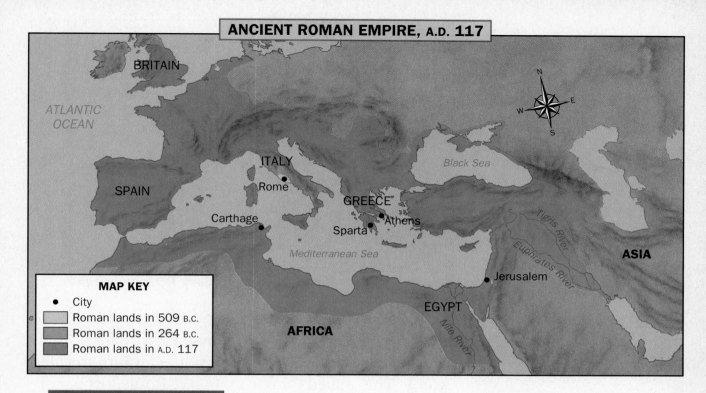

BRITAIN

ATLANTIC
OCEAN

SPAIN

ITALY

Rome

Carthage

GREECE

Sparta • Athens

Mediterranean Sea

Black Sea

Tigris River

Euphrates River

ASIA

Jerusalem

EGYPT

AFRICA

Nile River

MAP KEY
- City
  Roman lands in 509 B.C.
  Roman lands in 264 B.C.
  Roman lands in A.D. 117

Rome conquered many civilizations in Europe, Asia, and Africa. Which two civilizations in Africa did the Romans conquer?

Soldiers from Carthage

Both Rome and Carthage wanted to rule the land around the Mediterranean Sea. They fought each other for more than 100 years. In 146 B.C. Rome conquered Carthage. The Romans destroyed the city of Carthage. All the colonies of Carthage became Roman colonies. Then Rome conquered land to the east of the Mediterranean Sea. As the years passed, Rome ruled more and more land.

One of the greatest Romans was Julius Caesar. Julius Caesar became a leader of the Roman army. He conquered a lot of land in Europe for Rome. In 49 B.C. Julius Caesar was named ruler of Rome. He ruled Rome for five years.

Julius Caesar made many changes in Rome. He gave land to poor Romans. Many Romans did not have jobs. Julius Caesar gave these people jobs. People built new roads and temples for Rome. The new roads made it easier to travel through all the land that belonged to Rome. Julius Caesar gave the people in conquered lands the same rights that Romans had. After that, many conquered people wanted to help Rome.

Some roads that were built by the ancient Romans are still being used today.

Julius Caesar in Rome

Augustus Caesar

Many senators in Rome thought that Caesar had too much power. They did not want him to rule Rome. They killed Caesar in 44 B.C. Rome lost a strong leader.

Two men and their armies fought to rule Rome after Julius Caesar died. Augustus Caesar and Mark Antony both wanted to rule Rome. There was a war between them. Mark Antony lost the war. Augustus Caesar became the ruler of Rome.

Augustus Caesar was Rome's first emperor. He became emperor in the year 27 B.C. People do not vote for an emperor. Rome was no longer a republic. Rome was now an empire. Augustus was the one ruler of all the lands in the Roman Empire.

Augustus was a good emperor to his people. He made fair laws for the empire. While he ruled, many new cities were built in the empire. Many roads, bridges, and aqueducts were built all over the Roman Empire. He built a strong army. Augustus ruled for 41 years. Augustus brought peace to every part of the empire. This peace lasted 200 years.

Then the Roman Empire slowly grew weaker and weaker. How did that happen? You will learn the answer in the next chapter.

Using Vocabulary

Analogies An analogy compares two pairs of words. The words in the first pair are alike in the same way as the words in the second pair. For example, **pyramid** is to **Egypt** as **the Great Wall** is to **China**. Use a word in dark print to best complete each sentence. The first one is done for you.

aqueducts   innocent   republic   emperor   senator

1. A democracy was to Athens as a _____republic_____ was to Rome.

2. Pharaoh was to Egypt as _____ was to Rome.

3. Player is to team as _____ is to Senate.

4. Short is to tall as _____ is to guilty.

5. Roads are to people and goods as _____ are to water.

Read and Remember

Choose the Answer Draw a circle around the correct answer.

1. Where did the Roman Empire begin?

   Greece   Persia   Italy

2. When did people begin to build the city of Rome?

   753 B.C.   146 B.C.   27 B.C.

3. Who had most of the power in the Roman republic?

   kings   rich people   poor people

4. What city fought with Rome for the land around the Mediterranean Sea?

   Athens   Sparta   Carthage

5. Which Roman leader ruled for only five years before he was killed?

   Julius Caesar   Augustus Caesar   Mark Antony

6. Who became the first Roman emperor?

   Julius Caesar   Augustus Caesar   Mark Antony

Think and Apply

Exclusions   One word or phrase in each group does not belong. Find that word or phrase and cross it out. Then write on a separate sheet of paper a sentence that tells how the other words are alike.

1. Greece
Italy
Carthage
China

2. veto
democracy
fair trial
innocent until found guilty

3. bridges
pyramids
aqueducts
hospitals

4. Socrates
Julius Caesar
Augustus Caesar
Mark Antony

Skill Builder

Using Map Directions   Study the map on page 55. Find the compass rose. Then circle the word that best completes each sentence.

1. Spain is _____ of Italy.

north   west   south

2. Carthage is in the _____ part of Africa.

northern   eastern   western

3. The Black Sea is north of _____ .

the Atlantic Ocean   Britain   Egypt

4. In order to get from Rome to Jerusalem by boat, the Romans had to sail south and then _____ .

north   west   east

5. The Roman Empire included land as far _____ as Britain.

north   east   south

6. The _____ was in the southern part of the Roman Empire.

Tigris River   Black Sea   Nile River

Skill Builder

Reading a Resource Map   **Natural resources** are things we get from the earth. Metals such as iron, copper, and gold are natural resources. Foods and animals are also natural resources. A **resource map** uses symbols to show where different natural resources are found. The map key tells you what each symbol means. The resource map below shows where some natural resources were found in the Roman Empire around A.D. 117. Use the map and map key to answer the questions.

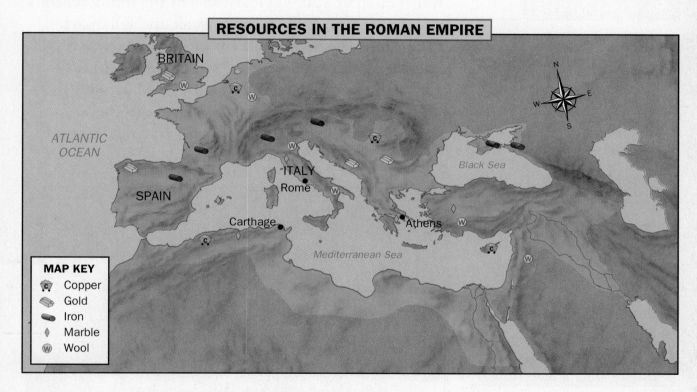

RESOURCES IN THE ROMAN EMPIRE

1. What five resources are shown on the map?_____

_____

2. What symbol is used to show wool?_____

3. What resource is found near Athens?_____

4. Did Romans get their wool from Spain or from Italy?_____

5. What two resources are found in Britain?_____

6. For which resource might the Romans have crossed the Black Sea?_____

The Fall of Rome

The Roman people lived in peace for 200 years. This peace began with Augustus Caesar. It ended in the year A.D. 180. Then the Roman Empire slowly grew weaker and weaker. In this chapter you will learn five of the many reasons why the Roman Empire grew weak and fell apart.

One reason the Roman Empire grew weak was that the empire was very large. The people in the conquered lands spoke many different languages. They lived far from the government in Rome. It was hard for the emperor in Rome to rule different people who were so far away.

The Roman Empire was conquered by people called barbarians.

Romans enjoyed watching fights in the Colosseum in Rome. You can see another picture of the Colosseum on page 43.

Wealthy Romans hunting

Roman coins

A second reason the Roman Empire grew weak was that it did not have good emperors. Many emperors who ruled after Augustus were not good rulers. They knew how to lead an army. But they did not make good laws.

The Roman Empire also grew weak because its army did not have enough good soldiers. Thousands of soldiers were needed for the huge empire. In the days of the Roman republic, the Roman soldiers had been proud to fight for Rome. The soldiers of the Roman Empire were different. Many of the empire's soldiers were from conquered lands. They were paid to fight for Rome. These soldiers did not care about Rome. They did not keep the empire strong.

A fourth reason the Roman Empire grew weak was because too many people were slaves. The rich people of Rome owned many slaves. Slaves were not paid for their work. Poor free people could not get jobs, since slaves were doing most of the work.

A fifth reason the Roman Empire grew weak was that it did not have enough money. It needed money for its huge army. It needed money to build cities and roads. Rome got the money it needed when people paid **taxes** to the emperor. As time passed,

The Roman Empire became divided. What were two cities in the Eastern Roman Empire?

fewer Romans had jobs. They were poor. They could pay very little taxes. The empire's slaves did not pay taxes at all. Rome did not have the money it needed to rule the empire. Rome grew weaker as the people grew poorer.

As Rome grew weaker, the people of the empire changed. The people of the Roman republic had been proud to be Romans and had worked hard for Rome. But the people of the Roman Empire were different. The rich did not work. They cared mostly about eating good meals and having fun. Most of the poor had lost their jobs. To keep the poor from making trouble, the emperor gave them free food and shows in the Colosseum in Rome. Few people cared about helping Rome. This made it easier for other people to conquer Rome.

Rome grew weaker and weaker during its last 200 years. The **population** of Rome became smaller. There were fewer people to protect the empire. At last, the empire was destroyed by different groups of people who had lived outside the Roman Empire.

These groups of people were called **barbarians**. They came from lands to the north, the west, and the east of the Roman Empire. They were farmers, hunters, and good fighters.

The barbarians invaded the Roman Empire again and again. Many of them came to live inside the empire. The weak Roman army could not keep the barbarians out. Then barbarians attacked the city of Rome. They would not let the Roman emperor rule. Barbarians became the rulers of Rome and began to rule different parts of the Roman Empire. The empire fell apart. This was called the **Fall of Rome**. Rome fell in A.D. 476.

Constantinople

Barbarians conquered only the western part of the empire in A.D. 476. The eastern part of the Roman Empire became known as the Byzantine Empire. The Byzantine Empire was strong until its fall in 1453. The main city of this empire was the city of Constantinople. It was located between the Mediterranean Sea and the Black Sea. This location made Constantinople an important trade center. The Byzantine Empire became rich from trade.

People from many cultures lived in the Byzantine Empire. They shared with each other their ideas about arts, science, building, and learning. The Byzantine Empire became a mixture of cultures.

One of the greatest Byzantine emperors was Justinian. He tried to unite the lands of the once strong Roman Empire. He also made many changes in the laws of the Byzantine Empire. Many of these laws are still used in many countries today. Justinian also had great churches built throughout the empire.

Justinian

The Romans gave the world fair laws, good roads, and fine buildings. After the Fall of Rome, the Byzantine Empire brought almost 1,000 years of learning and culture to the eastern part of Europe. But the Fall of Rome brought many hard years to the people who lived in the western part of the Roman Empire.

Empress Theodora (A.D. 502?–548)

Theodora was an important **empress** of the Byzantine Empire. She was married to Justinian. She had been an actress when she met Justinian. At that time it was against the law for government leaders to marry actresses. Justinian had the law changed so that he could marry Theodora. They married in 522. When Justinian became emperor in 527, Theodora became the empress.

Empress Theodora had many strong ideas about government, women, and religion. As empress she helped Justinian solve many government problems. She decided who would be given government and church jobs. She encouraged Justinian to build hospitals and churches. She also worked to give women more rights. Theodora even started homes to care for poor girls.

Empress Theodora

In 532 **riots** began between two groups of people. These people destroyed the city of Constantinople and tried to make another person the emperor. Justinian was going to give up his rule. But Theodora encouraged him to stay and fight. He and his soldiers stopped the riots. After the riots Justinian became an even stronger ruler than he had been before. He also worked to make Constantinople beautiful again.

In 542 a terrible **plague** made many people in Constantinople sick. Many people died. Justinian became sick. Theodora took his place as ruler of the Byzantine Empire until Justinian became well again. She was a strong and intelligent ruler. Even after Justinian was able to rule again, Theodora continued to make many government decisions. She and Justinian ruled together until her death in 548.

Using Vocabulary

Finish the Paragraph   Use the words in dark print to finish the paragraph below. Write on the correct blank lines the words you choose.

barbarians   **population**   **Fall of Rome**   **taxes**

There were many reasons why the Roman Empire grew weak. Its rulers did not make good laws. Many Romans were poor and could not pay their

_____ to the emperor. The empire did not have enough money

to rule. As Rome became weaker, the _____ of the empire

became lower. This meant there were fewer people to protect the empire. Many

people called _____ came from other lands and destroyed the

empire. Although the empire had once been great, these reasons led to the

_____ .

Read and Remember

Find the Answer   Put a check (✔) next to each sentence that tells a reason for the Fall of Rome. You should check four sentences.

_____ **1.** It was hard for the emperor in Rome to rule different people who were far away.

_____ **2.** Many emperors after Augustus were not good rulers.

_____ **3.** The Roman army did not have enough good soldiers.

_____ **4.** Only a few people were slaves.

_____ **5.** Barbarians invaded Rome from the north, the east, and the west.

_____ **6.** Constantinople was the main city in the Byzantine Empire.

_____ **7.** The Byzantine Empire was ruled by Justinian and Theodora.

Journal Writing

Theodora was an important Byzantine empress. Write a few sentences that explain some of the ways that Empress Theodora helped the Byzantine Empire.

Skill Builder

Reading a Line Graph   Graphs are drawings that help you compare facts. The graph below is a **line graph**. A line graph shows how something changes over time. The line graph below shows how the population of the city of Rome grew larger and smaller over the years of the Roman Empire. Study the graph. Then circle the correct answer to each question.

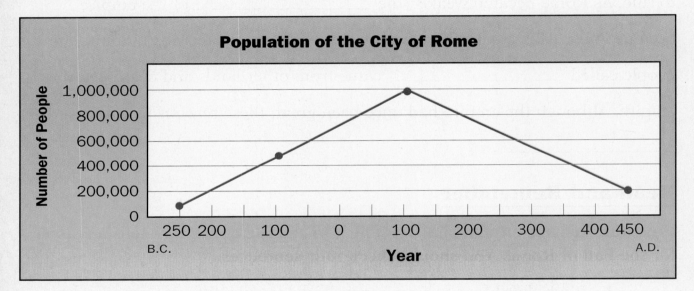

Population of the City of Rome

1. In which year did Rome have the largest population?

   100 B.C.   A.D. 100   A.D. 450

2. In which year did Rome have the smallest population?

   100 B.C.   A.D. 450   250 B.C.

3. In which year did Rome have about 500,000 people?

   250 B.C.   100 B.C.   A.D. 450

4. What might have led to the decrease of Rome's population after A.D. 100?

   better foods   barbarian invasions   good hospitals

CHAPTER 10

The Beginning of Christianity

THINK ABOUT AS YOU READ

1. **How did Christianity begin?**
2. **Why did many people want to become Christians?**
3. **How were churches in eastern Europe and in western Europe different?**

NEW WORDS

- New Testament
- Eastern Orthodox Church
- patriarch
- Roman Catholic Church
- pope

PEOPLE & PLACES

- Jesus
- Christians
- Theodosius

In Chapter 8 you learned that the Romans conquered land around the Mediterranean Sea. The Romans became the rulers of Palestine. A new religion began in Palestine while Augustus was the emperor of Rome.

The new religion was called Christianity. It began with a Jew named Jesus. He was born in Palestine. Jesus told people to believe in God. Some people did not forget Jesus when he died. These people believed Jesus was a great teacher. They also believed he was the Son of God, and they called him Jesus Christ. The people who believed in Jesus and his teachings became the first Christians.

In Chapter 4 you learned about a book called the Bible. The Old Testament and the **New Testament** are the two parts of the Christian Bible. The laws of

People who believed in the teachings of Jesus became Christians.

Lions attacking a Christian

Theodosius

Byzantine art of the baby Jesus

Moses and stories about the Jews of long ago are in the Old Testament. Stories about Jesus and his teachings are in the New Testament.

Many people of the Roman Empire became Christians. The Christians believed in only one god. This made many Roman emperors angry. The Roman emperors had many Christians killed. Some were killed by lions in the Colosseum. But the emperors could not stop people from becoming Christians.

Why did people want to be Christians? Most people in the Roman Empire were poor and lived hard lives. They wanted to believe that one day they would have a good life. Christians believed that they would live a happy life in heaven after they died. They also believed that God loved slaves and poor people as much as God loved rich people.

Theodosius was a Roman emperor who helped Christianity grow. In A.D. 392 he said that Christianity was the religion of the Roman Empire. Most people in the empire became Christians.

When the Roman Empire became divided, two different types of Christian churches developed. The Christians in eastern Europe became part of the **Eastern Orthodox Church**. Their church leaders were in Constantinople. The head of this church is called the **patriarch**. The Christians in western Europe became part of the **Roman Catholic Church**. Their church leaders were in Rome. The head of this church is called the **pope**.

The Fall of Rome in A.D. 476 brought many changes to the people of Europe. There were many hard years. The churches in eastern and western Europe became very powerful. The churches greatly affected every part of life in western Europe and in the Byzantine Empire. In the next chapter, you will learn more about life in Europe during the years after the Fall of Rome.

Using Vocabulary

Match Up   Finish the sentences in Group A with words from Group B. Write the letter of each correct answer on the blank line.

Group A

1. The teachings of Jesus are in the _____ of the Bible.

2. The head of the Eastern Orthodox Church is the _____ .

3. Church leaders in Rome were part of the _____ .

4. The head of the Roman Catholic Church is the _____ .

Group B

a. patriarch

b. New Testament

c. pope

d. Roman Catholic Church

Read and Remember

Finish the Sentence   Draw a circle around the word or words that best complete each sentence.

1. During the time of Jesus Christ, the _____ were the rulers of Palestine.

   Egyptians   Greeks   Romans

2. Jesus was a _____ .

   Jew   Hindu   Buddhist

3. Many people became Christians because they believed that God loved _____ people.

   only rich   only young   all

4. Emperor _____ said that Christianity was the religion of the Roman Empire.

   Augustus   Julius Caesar   Theodosius

5. The leaders of the Eastern Orthodox Church were in _____ .

   Athens   Rome   Constantinople

Skill Builder

Reading a Time Line   This time line shows some important events that happened before and after the birth of Jesus. Remember that when you count years before Jesus' birth (B.C.), the highest number tells you the oldest event. When you count years after Jesus' birth (A.D.), the lowest number tells you the oldest event. Read the events on the time line. Then write the answer to each question.

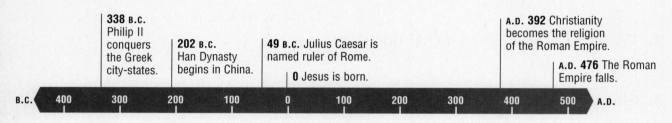

1. Which happened first: A.D. 200 or 200 B.C.? _____

2. Which happened last: 0 or 338 B.C.? _____

3. Which happened last: 100 B.C. or Julius Caesar becoming the ruler of Rome?

_____

4. Which happened first: the birth of Jesus or the beginning of the Han Dynasty

in China? _____

5. What happened in the year A.D. 476? _____

_____

6. In what year did Christianity become the religion of the Roman Empire?

_____

7. What is the oldest event on the time line? _____

_____

Journal Writing

Write a few sentences that explain how the Christian religion began and grew.

CHAPTER 11

Europe in the Middle Ages

THINK ABOUT AS YOU READ

1. **How did life in Europe change after the Fall of Rome?**
2. **What kinds of changes did Charlemagne make in Europe?**
3. **How did the feudal system help people in Europe during the Middle Ages?**

NEW WORDS

- ◆ Middle Ages
- ◆ feudalism
- ◆ feudal system
- ◆ nobles
- ◆ knights
- ◆ manor
- ◆ peasants
- ◆ castles

PEOPLE & PLACES

- ◆ Franks
- ◆ France
- ◆ Charlemagne

The years after the Fall of Rome were called the **Middle Ages**. The Middle Ages lasted about 1,000 years. They ended about the year 1500.

Life in western Europe was very different after the Fall of Rome. The once strong government of Rome disappeared. Europe was invaded again and again by the barbarians. The barbarians destroyed many cities and killed many people. Because of the barbarians, roads were not safe for traveling.

In the early Middle Ages, there were few schools in Europe. Most people could not read or write. There was little trade because of wars and dangerous roads. Without trade, towns and cities disappeared. People who had lived in towns and cities began farming. Most people tried to make or grow almost everything they needed.

During this time the Roman Catholic Church became very important in western Europe. People

Some manors had farms, a village, a church, and a castle.

Charlemagne

Charlemagne's Empire

Knights

were united by their belief in the Christian religion. The Church tried to encourage learning. The Church also collected taxes and made laws. The Roman Catholic Church grew rich and powerful.

The Franks were one group of barbarians. They conquered the land we now call France. In 768 a man named Charlemagne became the king of the Franks. Charlemagne conquered and ruled most of western Europe. He became the emperor of most of Europe by the year 800.

Charlemagne tried to make life better for the people he ruled. His army kept invaders out of Europe. He started many schools. He made many good laws and encouraged trade. Charlemagne spread Christianity throughout his empire. He also helped to increase the power of the Church.

After Charlemagne died, his sons became the rulers of the empire. They were weak rulers. They began to fight with each other to try to rule more land. Then Charlemagne's empire fell apart. Europe was divided into many kingdoms.

Europe was not safe after Charlemagne died. Barbarians began to invade Europe again. Rulers fought wars with each other. The kings of Europe did not have enough soldiers to protect their lands and people. Once again it was not safe to travel. It was not safe to live in cities. As people moved away from cities during the Middle Ages, a new way of living developed. It was called **feudalism**.

Feudalism was a system that helped the kings keep their lands and people safe. How did the **feudal system** work? A king gave large pieces of land to rich **nobles**. In return for the land, the nobles paid taxes to their king. The nobles also promised to fight for their king. Every noble had many soldiers. These soldiers were called **knights**. The knights worked to keep the land safe.

The nobles ruled the land that the king gave them. The land a noble ruled was called a **manor**.

Nobles built strong castles to protect the people on the manor.

THE FEUDAL SYSTEM

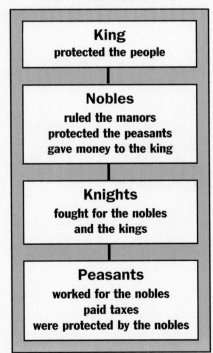

King
protected the people

Nobles
ruled the manors
protected the peasants
gave money to the king

Knights
fought for the nobles
and the kings

Peasants
worked for the nobles
paid taxes
were protected by the nobles

Sometimes a noble ruled many manors. The manor had farms, a church, and a village. Almost everything the people needed was made on the manor. Many people lived their whole lives on one manor. They had no reason to leave the manor. Many people left the cities of Europe and went to live on manors. Feudalism grew. It lasted for about 700 years.

Peasants were the largest part of the feudal system. Peasants were poor people. They lived on manors. They did the farm work. Peasants did all the hard work on the manor. They paid taxes to the noble who owned the manor. In return the noble protected the peasants and gave them small homes.

Nobles lived in large houses on the manor. Some nobles lived in **castles**. To keep safe, nobles built walls around their castles. The walls around the castles kept out invaders. If the manor was attacked, everyone would go into the castle to be safe.

Feudalism helped Europe become safer. There was less fighting. The feudal system gave the kings strong armies to protect their lands and people. The armies kept out the barbarian invaders. Roads were safer for travel. Soon people began moving into towns and cities again. By the 1200s feudalism was starting to become less important. Why did people want to live in towns and cities again? You will find the answer in Chapter 13.

Using Vocabulary

Finish Up   Choose the word or words in dark print that best complete each sentence. Write the word or words on the correct blank.

peasants   castles   knights   feudalism   Middle Ages

1. The years from the Fall of Rome to about 1500 were called the

_____ .

2. The system in Europe that was made up of the king, nobles, knights, and

peasants was known as _____ .

3. The _____ were poor people and were the largest group in the feudal system.

4. Some nobles built walls around large buildings called _____ to keep everyone on the manors safe.

5. Soldiers who fought for the nobles and kings were _____ .

Read and Remember

Write the Answer   Write one or more sentences to answer each question.

1. Why was the Roman Catholic Church important during the early

Middle Ages? _____

_____

2. What are three ways that Charlemagne helped Europe? _____

_____

_____

3. Under the feudal system, what did the nobles do for the king in return for land?

_____

Think and Apply

Drawing Conclusions   Read the first two sentences below. Then read the third sentence. Notice how it follows from the first two sentences. The third sentence is called a **conclusion**.

> Justinian tried to unite the lands of the Roman Empire.
> Justinian had many good laws that are still in use today.

CONCLUSION   Justinian was a strong ruler.

Read each pair of sentences. Then look in the box for the conclusion you might make. Write the letter of the conclusion on the blank. The first one is done for you.

1. After the Fall of Rome, the barbarians invaded western Europe often. Barbarians destroyed towns and cities all over western Europe.

   Conclusion ___c___

2. Charlemagne's army kept invaders out of Europe. Charlemagne made many good laws and started schools.

   Conclusion _____

3. Farms and villages were on the manor. Many people lived their whole lives on the manor.

   Conclusion _____

4. By the year 1200, Europe was a much safer place to live. People began to move into cities again.

   Conclusion _____

   a. Charlemagne tried to make life better for the people he ruled.
   b. Feudalism became less important.
   c. After the Fall of Rome, western Europe was not safe.
   d. People had everything they needed on the manor.

CHAPTER 12

Muslims and Their Empire

THINK ABOUT AS YOU READ

1. How did Islam begin?
2. How did Islam spread to other lands?
3. In what ways was the Muslim Empire a center of culture and learning during the Middle Ages?

NEW WORDS

♦ Islam
♦ prophet
♦ Allah
♦ Five Pillars of Islam
♦ Ramadan
♦ pilgrimage
♦ Koran
♦ mosques

PEOPLE & PLACES

♦ Muslims
♦ Muhammad
♦ Arabia
♦ Mecca
♦ Medina
♦ Spain
♦ Great Mosque
♦ Baghdad

A new religion began in the Middle East during the Middle Ages. This religion is called **Islam**. The people who believe in Islam are called Muslims. The Muslims conquered and ruled a great empire during the Middle Ages.

The story of Islam began with a man called Muhammad. Muhammad lived in Arabia. Arabia is a peninsula in the Middle East. Muhammad was born in the city of Mecca in the year A.D. 570.

Muhammad believed that he was God's **prophet**. A prophet is a person who believes that he or she is spoken to by God. A prophet tells others what God has said. Muhammad believed that Moses and Jesus were also prophets. Muhammad believed that he was the most important prophet.

Muhammad said that the name of God is **Allah**. He said that people must obey Allah by being kind and fair to each other. He also said that all Muslims must perform five duties. These duties are called the

Muslims have built beautiful mosques in which they pray to Allah.

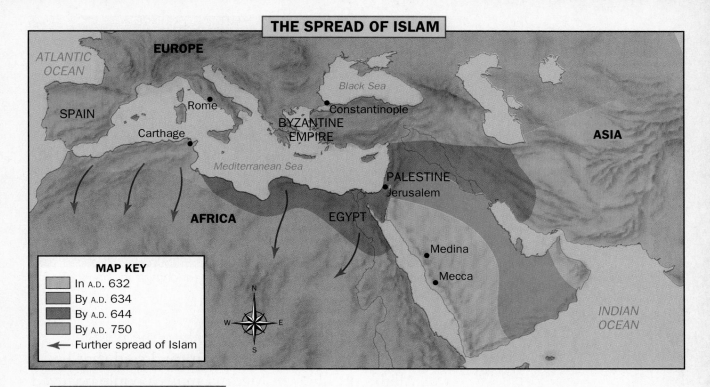

THE SPREAD OF ISLAM

EUROPE

ATLANTIC OCEAN

SPAIN

Rome

Carthage

Black Sea

Constantinople

BYZANTINE EMPIRE

ASIA

Mediterranean Sea

PALESTINE

Jerusalem

AFRICA

EGYPT

Medina

Mecca

INDIAN OCEAN

MAP KEY

In A.D. 632

By A.D. 634

By A.D. 644

By A.D. 750

← Further spread of Islam

N
W E
S

Muhammad taught that Muslims should face Mecca when they pray. In which direction would a Muslim in Egypt face to pray?

Muhammad

Five Pillars of Islam. The first duty is to make a statement about one's belief in Islam. This statement should be "There is no God but Allah, and Muhammad is His prophet." The second duty is to pray five times a day while facing Mecca. The third duty is to give money to help poor people. The fourth duty is to not eat or drink anything during the daylight hours of one month. This month is the Islamic month called **Ramadan**. The fifth duty is to make at least one **pilgrimage**, or journey, to Mecca.

The teachings of Muhammad are in a book called the **Koran**. Muslims in all parts of the world read and study the Koran. The Koran tells a person how to be a good Muslim.

A few people in Mecca believed what Muhammad said. These people became the first Muslims. They believed in Allah. However, at that time most people in Mecca believed in many gods. They wanted to stop Muhammad from teaching his new religion. Some of these people decided to kill him. In 622 Muhammad fled to the city of Medina to be safe.

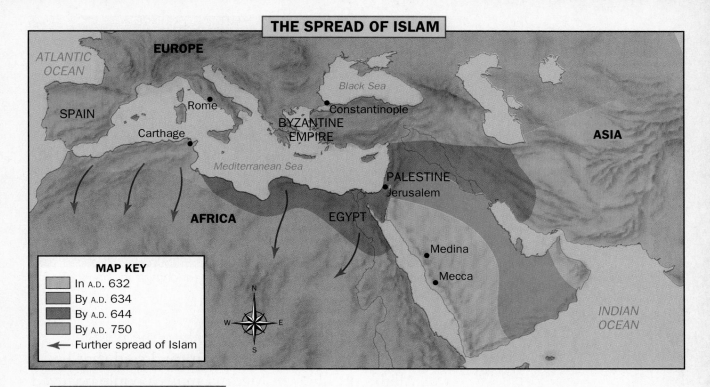

Muslims read and study Muhammad's teachings in the book called the Koran.

A page from the Koran

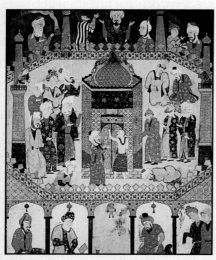

Muslims worshipping in Mecca

Muhammad spoke about Allah to the people of Medina. Again and again Muhammad said that he was Allah's prophet. In Medina many people believed what Muhammad said. Soon there were many Muslims in Medina.

Muhammad wanted everyone to believe in Islam. He said that people who fought and died for Islam would go to heaven. Many Muslims wanted to go to heaven when they died. So they became soldiers for Muhammad.

In 630 Muhammad and his soldiers conquered Mecca. Many people in Mecca became Muslims. Muhammad conquered all of Arabia. Islam became the religion of Arabia.

Muhammad died in the year 632. Muslims did not stop fighting for Islam after Muhammad died. Muslim soldiers fought in many lands. They conquered many countries. Many of the conquered people became Muslims.

The Muslims became the rulers of a large empire. The Muslims conquered the Middle East and northern Africa. They conquered the lands that are now Spain and Egypt. They ruled Persia and parts of India.

The Muslim Empire became a mixture of many cultures. Muslims learned much about science,

Millions of people from all over the world have gone to Mecca to pray in the Great Mosque.

A Muslim pilgrimage

math, and art from people in the conquered lands. Muslims also spread new ideas across the empire. The Muslim Empire became a center of culture during the Middle Ages. Many Muslims wrote poems and stories. They made beautiful works of art. The Muslims built great cities with beautiful buildings. Some of these great buildings were **mosques**. A mosque is a place where Muslims worship Allah. One of the most famous mosques is the Great Mosque in the city of Mecca.

The Muslim Empire also became a center of learning. The Muslims started many schools in cities such as Baghdad. They created new medicines and built hospitals. They studied the stars, the sun, and the moon. They used Hindu numbers to create new types of math.

After 200 years the Muslim Empire grew weaker. Muslim leaders began to fight with each other. Different people became rulers of different parts of the empire. The empire fell apart. But Islam continues to be one of the world's great religions.

There are millions of Muslims in the world today. They believe in the religion Muhammad started in Arabia over a thousand years ago. The culture and the history of Islam unite Muslims all over the world.

USING WHAT YOU LEARNED

Using Vocabulary

Find the Meaning   Write on the blank the word or words that best complete each sentence.

1. A **pilgrimage** is a _____.

   journey   saying   soldier

2. Muslims believe that **Allah** is the name of _____.

   Muhammad   Islam   God

3. The **Koran** is a book of the teachings of _____.

   Confucius   Allah   Muhammad

4. **Ramadan** is an Islamic _____ in which Muslims do not eat or drink during the day.

   week   month   year

Read and Remember

Finish the Paragraph   Use the words in dark print to finish the paragraph below. Write on the correct blank lines the words you choose.

religion	Mecca	Five Pillars	mosques
culture	Muslims	Muhammad	

Islam began with a man called _____. He said that people must perform duties called the _____ of Islam. One of the duties is to pray five times a day facing _____. The people who believed Muhammad's teachings became _____. These people conquered Mecca and all of Arabia. Islam became the _____ of Arabia. The Muslim Empire became a center of _____ during the Middle Ages. Muslims made beautiful works of art and built _____ for praying to Allah.

Think and Apply

Sequencing Events   Write the numbers **1, 2, 3, 4,** and **5** next to these sentences to show the correct order.

_____ Muhammad and his soldiers conquered Mecca in 630.

_____ Muslims became the rulers of a large empire.

_____ Muhammad fled Mecca in 622 and went to Medina.

_____ The Muslim Empire became weak because Muslim leaders began to fight with each other.

_____ Muhammad began to tell his ideas about Allah to people in Mecca.

Skill Builder

Using Intermediate Map Directions
In Chapter 1 you learned about the four main directions—north, south, east, and west. Some compass roses also show four **intermediate,** or in-between, directions. They are **northeast, southeast, southwest,** and **northwest**. For example, southeast is between south and east. Study the map on page 77. Circle the direction that best finishes each sentence.

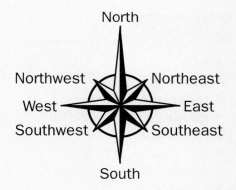

1. Jerusalem is _____ of Constantinople.

southeast   west   northeast

2. When Muhammad fled from Mecca to Medina, he traveled _____ .

northeast   southwest   northwest

3. According to the map, Islam first spread to the _____ .

northeast   south   northwest

4. The Mediterranean Sea is _____ of the Indian Ocean.

northeast   southeast   northwest

CHAPTER 13

The Growth of Cities and Trade

There were many changes in Europe between the years 1000 and 1500. Europe's population increased. More people began to live in cities. Arts and learning increased. People began to trade more with each other. Europeans could buy things from far-off places like Asia and the Middle East. How did these changes happen?

You have learned that Muslims from Arabia conquered the Middle East. They conquered Palestine in the 600s. For many years the Muslims let Christians go to the city of Jerusalem in Palestine. Christians made pilgrimages to Jerusalem. Jerusalem is a **holy** city for Christians, Jews, and Muslims. However, during the 1000s Muslims called Turks conquered Palestine, the Byzantine Empire, and other parts of Asia. They won control of Jerusalem in 1071. The Turks would not let Christians go to Jerusalem.

As you learned in Chapter 10, the leader of the Roman Catholic Church is called the pope. In 1095

THINK ABOUT AS YOU READ

1. What were the Crusades?
2. How did the Crusades change life in Europe?
3. Why did people want to move to cities?

NEW WORDS

♦ holy
♦ Crusades
♦ recaptured
♦ goods
♦ merchant
♦ woodblock printing
♦ spices
♦ diseases

PEOPLE & PLACES

♦ Europeans
♦ Turks
♦ Pope Urban II
♦ Crusaders
♦ the East
♦ Marco Polo
♦ Venice
♦ Italian

As towns and cities grew, they became centers for buying and selling goods.

Christians fought the Crusades to recapture Palestine from the Turks.

Crusaders fighting Turks

Marco Polo

Pope Urban II told Europeans that they should fight wars to free Palestine from the Turks. Thousands of Christians decided to fight for Palestine.

The Christian wars to capture Palestine were called the **Crusades**. The Crusades were fought in the late Middle Ages. The Christian soldiers who fought in these wars were called Crusaders. Not all Crusaders cared about winning Palestine for the pope. Many Crusaders wanted to win new lands and riches for themselves. Others wanted to open up trade with the Middle East.

The Crusades lasted almost 200 years. The Crusaders captured Jerusalem in the year 1099. Christians ruled Jerusalem for almost ninety years. Then the Turks **recaptured** Jerusalem. By 1291 the Muslims ruled all of Palestine again. The Crusaders were not able to recapture Palestine.

The Crusaders learned about new foods and clothing from the Muslims. The Crusaders brought food, cloth, and new ideas back to Europe. Soon Europeans wanted more **goods** from Asia and the Middle East. Asia and the Middle East were often called the East. Trade increased between Europe and the East.

A man named Marco Polo helped Europeans learn more about the East. Marco Polo was the son of a **merchant**. In 1271 Marco was 17 years old. That year he, his father, and his uncle left Italy and

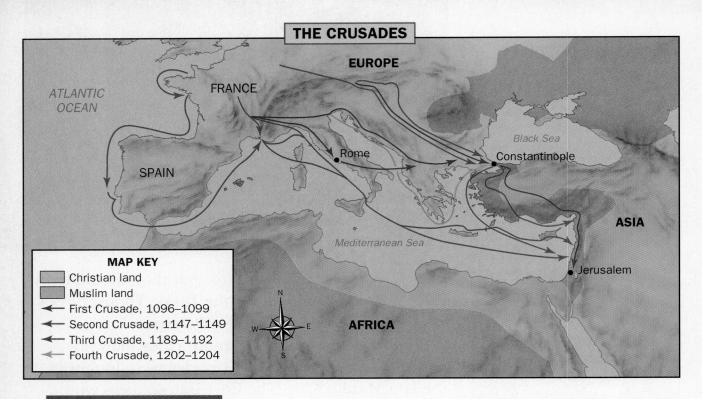

THE CRUSADES

EUROPE

ATLANTIC OCEAN

FRANCE

SPAIN

Rome

Black Sea

Constantinople

ASIA

Mediterranean Sea

Jerusalem

AFRICA

MAP KEY
- Christian land
- Muslim land
- First Crusade, 1096–1099
- Second Crusade, 1147–1149
- Third Crusade, 1189–1192
- Fourth Crusade, 1202–1204

Crusaders took many different routes to Jerusalem. Which Crusades crossed the Mediterranean Sea to reach Jerusalem?

Chinese printing block

began their trip across Asia to China. It took almost four years to reach China.

Marco Polo liked what he saw and learned in China. China had an advanced civilization. Many inventions were made in China during the Middle Ages. In the 700s the Chinese invented **woodblock printing**. It was much faster to use woodblock printing to make books than to write books by hand. Europeans would not begin to use woodblock printing until the 1200s.

Marco Polo stayed in China until 1292. During that time he learned to speak the language of China. He traveled all over China. He also worked for the Chinese emperor. When Marco Polo returned to Italy in 1295, he brought many beautiful things with him. He wrote a book about his trip. People read about China. Soon many people wanted to learn more about other far-off lands.

The Crusades and Marco Polo helped trade grow between Europe and the East. Ships carried goods to and from different cities in Europe. Other ships carried goods to the Middle East and Asia.

People bought and sold goods in the Italian city-state of Venice.

Grain and spices

Ships brought foods, silk, **spices**, and other goods from the East back to Europe. Venice and other Italian city-states became important trading centers.

Trade brought other changes to Europe. One change was that money became important. People began to use money to buy and sell goods. Another change was that merchants became an important group of people. As time passed, many merchants grew rich and powerful. A third change was that towns and cities became important.

Towns and cities were good places for buying, selling, and storing goods. Many new towns and cities were started. Most cities were built near seas or rivers. Many of these cities became rich trading centers. Cities grew quickly during the Middle Ages. However, people did not carefully plan most cities. City streets were narrow and dirty. Garbage was thrown in the streets. Houses were built close together. There were many fires. Fires moved quickly from one house to another house.

The crowded, dirty cities also made it easier for **diseases** to spread. One terrible disease was the plague. The plague spread quickly through many cities in Europe and Asia during the Middle Ages. The plague became known as the Black Death. It killed millions of people.

Doctor visiting a man with the plague

During the Middle Ages, people in Europe built many great churches called cathedrals.

Narrow streets in a crowded European city

But even though cities had many problems, many people wanted to live in cities. Cities had churches and schools. There were many kinds of jobs in cities. Many people thought they could have a better life in cities.

Feudalism ended because of the growth of cities. City people had to pay taxes to the king. Now kings had money to pay soldiers to fight for them. The nobles became less important. The kings had more power. Many peasants ran away from manors to go to cities. They had hard lives on the manors. They hoped to find better jobs in cities. As time passed, fewer people lived on manors. More and more people lived in towns and cities. Feudalism slowly ended.

The Middle Ages ended about the year 1500. By then, many people were living and working in towns and cities. Some people were making goods for merchants to buy and sell. Merchants were trading goods in far-off lands. Kings were becoming more powerful. In the years ahead, many more changes would come to Europe.

Using Vocabulary

Finish the Paragraph   Use the words in dark print to finish the paragraph below. Write on the correct blank lines the words you choose.

goods   merchants   spices   Crusades

There were many changes in Europe during the years 1000 to 1500.

Christians and Turks fought in the _____ for the control of

the holy city of Jerusalem. These wars helped increase trade with the East.

The Crusaders brought back to Europe many _____, such as

foods and cloth. They also brought back _____ to add to their

foods. As trade and money became important, many _____ who

traded with the East became rich and powerful. Cities also became important.

Read and Remember

Finish Up   Choose the word or words in dark print to best complete each sentence. Write the word or words on the correct blank line.

woodblock   Pope Urban II   riches   plague   Marco Polo

1. Many Crusaders wanted to win new lands and _____ for themselves.

2. In 1095 _____ told Europeans to fight the Muslims in the Crusades.

3. _____ wrote a book about what he saw and learned in China.

4. The Chinese method of _____ printing was faster than writing books by hand.

5. The _____ spread quickly through dirty, crowded cities during the Middle Ages.

Think and Apply

Fact or Opinion   Write **F** next to each fact below. Write **O** next to each opinion. You should find two sentences that are opinions.

_____ **1.** The Turks recaptured Jerusalem from the Christians.

_____ **2.** The Crusaders learned many new ideas from the Muslims.

_____ **3.** Marco Polo was very smart.

_____ **4.** Venice became an important trading center during the Middle Ages.

_____ **5.** It was easier to live on a manor than to live in a city.

Skill Builder

Reading a Bar Graph   A **bar graph** shows facts using bars of different lengths. The bar graph below shows how the population in the countryside was divided in England about 1086. England is a country of Europe. Study the graph. Then write the answer to each question.

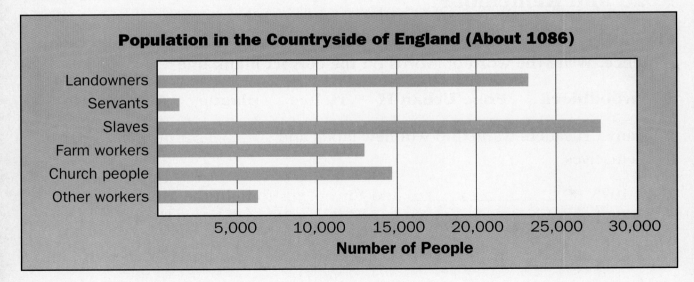

Population in the Countryside of England (About 1086)

Landowners
Servants
Slaves
Farm workers
Church people
Other workers

5,000   10,000   15,000   20,000   25,000   30,000
Number of People

1. What group of people was the largest? _____

2. What group was the smallest? _____

3. Which group had about 13,000 people? _____

4. About how many church people were there? _____

Crossword Puzzle

Each sentence below has a word missing. Choose the missing word for each sentence from the words in dark print. Then write the words in the correct places on the puzzle.

―――――――――――――――― **ACROSS** ――――――――――――――――

Crusaders   trade   Turks   money

1. During the Middle Ages, people began to use _____ to buy and sell goods.

2. The _____ were Christian soldiers who wanted to capture Palestine.

3. After the Crusades, Europeans began to _____ with people in the East.

4. The _____ were Muslims who conquered Palestine.

―――――――――――――――― **DOWN** ――――――――――――――――

garbage   merchants   seas   feudal

5. People who buy and sell goods are called _____ .

6. People in cities threw _____ in the streets.

7. As cities grew, the _____ system ended.

8. Many cities were built near _____ .

Unit 3 The Growth of Nations and Ideas

How would a map look that showed the world in the year 1000? The lands and the oceans of today's world would be on the map. But today's nations would not be on the old world map. Before the year 1000, there were no nations in the world. After the year 1000, nations began to form. England, France, Spain, and other nations became strong. Great civilizations in Africa and the Americas also grew during this time.

The years between 1000 and 1800 were years of growth in Europe and other parts of the world. Europe did not grow larger in size. It grew in many other ways. There was a growth of new ideas in Europe. These ideas made learning important again. Art became more important. New ideas about democracy grew in England. The Roman Catholic Church became less powerful, and some people started new kinds of churches.

The number of explorers grew during this time. Many explorers from Europe wanted to find new and better ways to go to Asia. The nations of Europe started colonies in Asia, Africa, and the Americas. The number of colonies increased.

How did nations form after the year 1000? What civilizations were in Africa and in the Americas? Why did learning and democracy

PACIFIC OCEAN

ATLANTIC OCEAN

PACIFIC OCEAN

INDIAN OCEAN

become more important? Why did nations want colonies? As you read Unit 3, think about how nations are different from city-states and from empires. Think about how different our world might have been without explorers or new ideas.

	1200 The Aztec and Inca empires begin.	**1453** France wins the Hundred Years' War.	**1689** The English Bill of Rights is written.
1000 Ghana is a strong empire. Zimbabwe is built.	**1307** Mansa Musa becomes the king of Mali.	**1519** Magellan sails around South America.	**1763** Great Britain wins the French and Indian War.

A.D. 1000 — 1100 — 1200 — 1300 — 1400 — 1500 — 1600 — 1700 — 1800

1200–1700
Growth of democracy in England

1300–1600
Renaissance in Europe

CHAPTER 14

New Nations Begin

THINK ABOUT AS YOU READ

1. **What is a nation?**
2. **How did kings become more powerful than nobles?**
3. **How did England, France, and Spain become nations?**

NEW WORDS

♦ nations
♦ monarchs
♦ isolation
♦ monarchy
♦ Hundred Years' War
♦ battles
♦ executed

PEOPLE & PLACES

♦ United States
♦ Americans
♦ English
♦ English Channel
♦ William the Conqueror
♦ French
♦ Joan of Arc
♦ Orléans
♦ King Ferdinand V
♦ Queen Isabella

As the years of the Middle Ages passed, many changes occurred in Europe. Feudalism was ending. Kings in Europe were becoming more powerful. Kings began to unite the people of their lands. As people in lands united, they formed **nations**.

Nations are made up of people who have the same laws and leaders. Often people of one nation speak the same language. Our nation is the United States. The people of the United States are called Americans. Most Americans speak the English language. They obey American laws.

During the early years of the Middle Ages, there were no nations in Europe. Most people lived on manors. Every manor was ruled by a different noble. The noble made laws for the manor. **Monarchs** had little power. A monarch is a king or a queen.

The growth of cities and trade helped feudalism end. It also helped monarchs become strong rulers.

Barbarians came by sea to invade England.

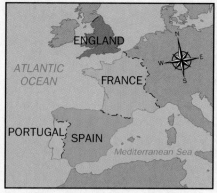
Four Nations in the Middle Ages

William the Conqueror

William and his soldiers conquered England.

There was more money in Europe. People paid taxes to the monarchs. The monarchs had money to build large armies. The armies helped the monarchs become even more powerful. They began to have more control over people in their lands. As time passed, monarchs ruled more and more land. People who lived on this land had to obey the laws of their king or queen.

How did England become a nation? Look at the map on this page. You can see that England is on an island. It is separated from the rest of Europe by the English Channel. This **isolation** helped England become a nation.

In A.D. 43 England was invaded by the Romans. Then in the 400s, barbarians invaded England. They brought new ideas to England. During the Middle Ages, the people of England lived on manors. They were ruled by nobles.

England was invaded again in 1066. A noble from an area of northern France invaded England. His name was William the Conqueror. William and his soldiers were good fighters. They conquered England. William the Conqueror became the king of England.

William was a strong king. He helped England become a **monarchy**. A monarchy is a nation where the monarch has all the power to rule. Everyone in England had to obey William's laws. After William died, different monarchs ruled England for many years. They helped England become one nation.

How did France become a nation? France had also been part of the Roman Empire. Then, as you learned in Chapter 11, barbarians called Franks ruled France. When Charlemagne became king, he gained much power in France. But before and after Charlemagne, kings did not have much power.

During the Middle Ages, France was made up of many states. Some states were ruled by nobles. Other states in France were ruled by England. About the year 1000, French kings began to take land away from

The French freed the city of Orléans from the English during the Hundred Years' War.

Joan of Arc

the nobles. They also wanted the lands in France that were ruled by England. They wanted France to become a strong country.

The English and the French fought in France. They fought for over 100 years. Their fight was called the **Hundred Years' War**. This war helped France become a nation. The war began in 1337.

A young woman named Joan of Arc helped France win the Hundred Years' War. Joan believed that God wanted her to lead the French army against the English. She told the French king. He believed her and gave her a small army.

The English were ruling the French city of Orléans. Joan of Arc led the French army to fight for Orléans. They freed the city of Orléans from the English. But the war had not ended. The English and the French kept on fighting. Joan won other **battles**. Then the English captured Joan of Arc. She was **executed** by the English.

Joan of Arc made the French feel proud to fight for France. The French kept fighting after Joan died. In 1453 the French won the war. England lost most of its land in France.

King Ferdinand V

Queen Isabella

A Muslim building in Spain

France was a powerful monarchy by the end of the Middle Ages. French states were no longer ruled by nobles. Every state was ruled by the king of France. Everyone had to obey the French king and the king's laws.

Spain also became a nation during the Middle Ages. Like England and France, Spain had been ruled by the Romans and then by the barbarians. Then in the 700s, the Muslims conquered and ruled most of Spain. Many people in Spain were Roman Catholics. They did not want to be ruled by Muslims. Roman Catholics fought against the Muslims for about 500 years. Slowly the Catholics recaptured parts of Spain from the Muslims.

At that time Spain was made up of four states. In 1469 King Ferdinand V ruled one state. Queen Isabella ruled another state. Their states were joined when the king and queen married. Later the king and queen became the rulers of the other two states. King Ferdinand V and Queen Isabella led the fight against the Muslims. In 1492 the Catholics won the war against the Muslims. Then Catholics ruled all of Spain.

Spain became a monarchy. King Ferdinand V and Queen Isabella ruled the nation. They made laws for all the people of Spain. One law said that everyone in Spain had to be Catholic. Muslims and Jews had to either leave Spain or become Catholics. People who were not Catholics were punished or killed. King Ferdinand V and Queen Isabella took power away from nobles and church leaders. They became powerful rulers. Spain was becoming an important nation.

England, France, and Spain became nations during the Middle Ages. Each nation had its own language, laws, and monarchs. Many other nations were also beginning. You will read about some of these nations in later chapters.

Using Vocabulary

Analogies   Use the words in dark print to best complete the sentences.

monarchy   **isolation**   **Hundred Years' War**   **monarchs**

1. The English Channel was to _____ in England as the Great Wall was to protection in China.

2. Pharaohs were to ancient Egypt as _____ were to England, France, and Spain during the Middle Ages.

3. A _____ was to England, France, and Spain as a dynasty was to ancient China.

4. Christian soldiers were to the Crusades as Joan of Arc was to the

_____ .

Read and Remember

Choose the Answer   Draw a circle around the correct answer.

1. What separated England from France and the rest of Europe?

   Indian Ocean   Mediterranean Sea   English Channel

2. From where did William the Conqueror come?

   northern France   Spain   Italy

3. For which nation did Joan of Arc and her soldiers win an important battle in the Hundred Years' War?

   England   France   Spain

4. Which nation did King Ferdinand V and Queen Isabella rule after they won the war against the Muslims?

   England   France   Spain

5. Which people in Spain were punished or killed because of their religion?

   Christians   Catholics   Muslims

Think and Apply

Compare and Contrast   Read each sentence below. Decide whether it tells about England, France, or Spain. Write **E** next to each sentence that tells about England. Write **F** next to each sentence that tells about France. Write **S** next to each sentence that tells about Spain.

_____ **1.** The Muslims conquered this land in the Middle Ages.

_____ **2.** This nation was conquered by a French noble who then became the king.

_____ **3.** This nation won the battle at the city of Orléans.

_____ **4.** A law in this nation said that all people had to be Catholic.

Skill Builder

Reading a Chart   Read the chart below about three new nations. Then write the answer to each question.

THREE NEW NATIONS

Nation	Date	Events
England	1066	William the Conqueror invaded England and became king. England became one nation.
France	1453	France won the Hundred Years' War. England lost most of its land in France.
Spain	1492	Catholics won the war against Muslims. The states of Spain became one nation under King Ferdinand V and Queen Isabella.

1. When did William the Conqueror invade England?_____

2. What states became one nation in 1492?_____

3. What happened when France won the Hundred Years' War?_____

_____

4. Which was the first to become a nation: Spain, England, or France?_____

_____

The Growth of Democracy

The monarchs of Europe were powerful leaders. They believed that God gave them the right to be rulers. The monarchs believed they should make all the laws. Everyone had to obey the monarchs. England was one of the first countries in Europe where monarchs became less powerful. In this chapter you will learn how England slowly became a democracy.

Democracy means rule by the people. Democracy was a powerful idea. It changed the way monarchs ruled their nations. In a democracy people have a voice in their government. In a democracy people

NEW WORDS

- ♦ **Magna Carta**
- ♦ **prison**
- ♦ **defeat**
- ♦ **jury**
- ♦ **broken the law**
- ♦ **Parliament**
- ♦ **middle class**
- ♦ **House of Lords**
- ♦ **House of Commons**
- ♦ **Bill of Rights**
- ♦ **freedom of speech**

PEOPLE & PLACES

- ♦ **King John**
- ♦ **King Edward I**
- ♦ **John Locke**

Nobles in England wanted King John to have less power, so they forced him to sign the Magna Carta.

Magna Carta

King John

People paying taxes

vote for their leaders. People vote for men and women who will make their laws. It took hundreds of years for England to become a democracy. It took even longer for democracy to begin in other nations.

In Chapter 7 you read about the world's first democracy. It began in Athens. When Athens was conquered, that democracy ended. During the Middle Ages, people did not rule themselves. They were ruled by powerful nobles and monarchs.

In Chapter 14 you read that William the Conqueror became king of England in 1066. He was a powerful king. But William did not make the laws by himself. He asked a group of nobles and church leaders to help him. Groups of nobles and church leaders also helped the kings who ruled after William. By the year 1300, less powerful people also helped the kings make laws. This was a small step toward democracy.

Another step toward democracy was the **Magna Carta**. The Magna Carta was a paper that said the king must obey the laws. It said a king could not make all the tax laws by himself. It also said that the king could not send people to **prison** just because he did not like them. The king no longer had full power. The Magna Carta was signed by King John, who ruled England from 1199 to 1216. A group of nobles forced King John to sign the Magna Carta in 1215.

Why did King John have to sign the Magna Carta? The nobles in England did not like King John or his taxes. King John often did not obey the laws of England. The nobles wanted King John to have less power. So they wrote the Magna Carta. The nobles said they would not pay any more taxes unless King John signed the Magna Carta. At first King John would not sign. The nobles put together a big army. King John knew he could not **defeat** the nobles' army. He also needed tax money. So he signed the Magna Carta.

How did the Magna Carta change England? Before the Magna Carta, the king could send anyone to prison. After the Magna Carta, an accused person could not be sent to prison without a trial by **jury**. A jury is a group of people who hear information about an accused person and the crime. Then the jury decides if the accused person has **broken the law**. Today in a democracy, every accused person has the right to a jury trial.

Parliament building

After the Magna Carta was signed, the king could no longer make tax laws by himself. The king worked with a group of people to make laws. This group became known as **Parliament**. When the king wanted people to pay more taxes, he had to ask members of Parliament. They decided whether the people should pay more taxes.

Parliament became important in England. The king no longer had full power. The king had to obey the laws of Parliament. The king could not get tax money without Parliament's help. Parliament brought England closer to democracy.

At first only nobles worked in Parliament. In 1295 people from the **middle class** began to work in Parliament also. In that year King Edward I divided Parliament into two parts. The nobles in Parliament worked in the part called the **House of Lords**. The other part of Parliament was called the **House of Commons**. Middle-class people worked in the House of Commons. Most people in England were not nobles. England moved closer to democracy as the House of Commons became more powerful. After hundreds of years, the House of Commons was more powerful than the House of Lords.

King Edward I

The English **Bill of Rights** of 1689 brought England closer to democracy. It made Parliament more powerful than the English monarch. The Bill of Rights gave Parliament more power to make laws. All tax laws would be written by Parliament. The Bill of Rights gave **freedom of speech** in Parliament to the English people. This means people were allowed to speak in Parliament against the government. The

In 1295 King Edward I divided Parliament into two parts. He is shown here with the House of Lords.

John Locke

Bill of Rights also said that people have a right to a fair and speedy trial. Kings and queens in England ruled together with Parliament.

A man named John Locke helped spread the ideas of democracy. John Locke lived most of his life in England. In 1690 he wrote about his ideas. He wrote that people should choose their rulers. He wrote that people have the right to make laws for themselves. Governments must help and protect people. Locke wrote that kings should not be powerful rulers. Many people liked John Locke's ideas. His ideas helped England's Parliament become stronger. Other nations used Locke's ideas to become democracies.

While England was becoming a democracy, many other changes were taking place in Europe. How were other parts of Europe changing? The answers are in Chapter 16.

Using Vocabulary

Finish Up   Choose words in dark print to finish each sentence. Write the words on the correct blank line.

freedom of speech   **middle class**
House of Lords   **Bill of Rights**

1. People in the _____ were not as rich as nobles or as poor as peasants.

2. The English _____ of 1689 was a paper that gave more power to Parliament and more rights to the English people.

3. The right of _____ gave people the right to speak out against the government.

4. Nobles worked in a part of Parliament called the _____ .

Read and Remember

Who Am I?   Read each sentence. Then look at the words in dark print for the name of the person who might have said it. Write on the blank after each sentence the name of the person you choose.

King John   **William the Conqueror**   **John Locke**   **King Edward I**

1. "I ruled England from 1066 and asked nobles and church leaders to help write the laws." _____

2. "The nobles would not pay more taxes until I gave up some of my power."

_____

3. "I divided Parliament into two parts so that both the nobles and the middle class could make laws." _____

4. "I wrote that people should be able to choose their rulers and make laws for themselves." _____

Think and Apply

Categories   Read the words in each group. Decide how they are alike. Find the best title for each group from the words in dark print. Write the title on the line above each group.

Democracy   **Parliament**   **King John**   **Magna Carta**

1. _____
   made high taxes
   had too much power
   signed the Magna Carta

2. _____
   trial by jury
   written by nobles
   king lost power

3. _____
   citizens vote
   first began in Athens
   Parliament made laws

4. _____
   writes England's laws
   House of Commons
   House of Lords

Skill Builder

Reading a Population Map
A **population map** shows the number of people living in different places. The map key of a population map gives colors or patterns for different numbers of people. This map shows how many people per square mile were living in Europe in 1300. Study the map. Then write the answer to each question below.

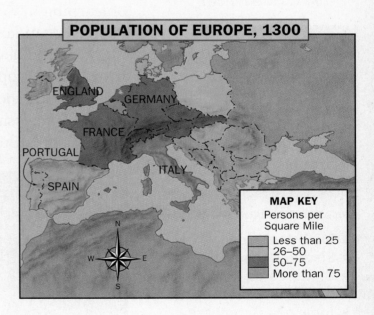

POPULATION OF EUROPE, 1300

ENGLAND
GERMANY
FRANCE
PORTUGAL
ITALY
SPAIN

MAP KEY
Persons per Square Mile
Less than 25
26–50
50–75
More than 75

1. What color shows less than 25 people per square mile?_____

2. How many people per square mile lived in England in 1300?_____

3. Did France, Spain, or Italy have more people per square mile in 1300?

The Renaissance

In 1508 the pope gave the artist Michelangelo an important job. The artist was asked to paint the ceiling of a large church in Rome. For four long years, Michelangelo painted the ceiling of the famous Sistine Chapel. He lay flat on his back on top of a high platform as he painted the ceiling. Michelangelo painted pictures that told stories from the Bible. You can see part of this famous work on page 91. Michelangelo was one of the great artists of the **Renaissance**.

The word *Renaissance* means "to be born again," or "**rebirth**." During the Renaissance there was a rebirth of learning in Europe. There was a rebirth of art. People began learning more about science and math. They created new kinds of music. They wrote new **literature**. People asked many questions about the world during the Renaissance. New ideas were born.

The Renaissance began about the year 1300 in Italy. It spread to other countries in Europe in the

THINK ABOUT AS YOU READ

1. **What was the Renaissance?**
2. **How did the Renaissance change Europe?**
3. **Who were some of the important people in the Renaissance?**

NEW WORDS

♦ **Renaissance**
♦ **rebirth**
♦ **literature**
♦ **religious**
♦ **Scientific Revolution**
♦ **movable type**

PEOPLE & PLACES

♦ **Michelangelo**
♦ **Sistine Chapel**
♦ **Leonardo da Vinci**
♦ **Tarquinia Molza**
♦ **Johannes Gutenberg**
♦ **William Shakespeare**
♦ **Elizabeth I**
♦ **Henry VIII**
♦ **Anne Boleyn**
♦ **Spanish**

Lorenzo de Medici was a wealthy man who spent much of his money on Renaissance art and buildings.

Renaissance artists sometimes painted pictures about daily life. Here peasants enjoy a wedding feast.

Michelangelo

Michelangelo's statue *David*

late 1400s. The Renaissance lasted about 300 years. It brought important changes to Europe.

What was Europe like before the Renaissance? Before the Renaissance, religion was very important in Europe. People were concerned about going to heaven after they died. Most artists painted only **religious** pictures. Schools in Europe were usually part of churches. Most people did not go to school and could not read or write.

The Renaissance changed Europe. Although religion was still important, people stopped waiting for a good life in heaven. People wanted to enjoy life on earth before they died. Artists painted religious pictures as well as many other kinds of pictures. They tried to find new and better ways to make paintings and statues. Learning became important. Many schools were started. More people went to school.

During the Renaissance, people studied works of art from ancient Greece and Rome. They used ideas from long ago to make new works of art. They also wrote new kinds of literature.

The Renaissance first began in Italy. There are many reasons why it began there. Italy was the center of world trade at that time. Ships from Italy went to

Leonardo da Vinci

Da Vinci's painting *Mona Lisa*

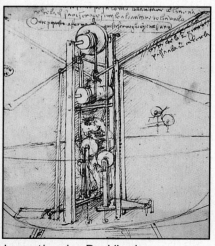

Invention by Da Vinci

Africa and Asia. People brought back to Italy ideas from Asia and Africa. Artists and writers used these ideas to create new kinds of work. The Roman Catholic Church also encouraged arts and learning.

Rich people in Italy gave artists money so that the artists could work. The pope and the Roman Catholic Church also gave artists money to do their work. This helped the growth of art in Italy.

Italy was a center of learning. People from other parts of Europe came to Italy to study with great artists. These people brought ideas from Italy back to other parts of Europe. The Renaissance slowly spread to England, France, Spain, and many other parts of Europe.

Leonardo da Vinci was one of the greatest people of the Renaissance. He lived in Italy. He became one of the world's great artists. His painting *Mona Lisa* became very famous. Da Vinci did more than paint well. He also knew a lot about math and science. He drew pictures for new inventions. He also drew plans for new buildings. Da Vinci was called a "Renaissance Man" because he did so many different things well.

There were also famous women in the Renaissance. Some rich women gave money to artists and writers. Some women were artists. Their paintings are still enjoyed today. One woman, Tarquinia Molza, was a "Renaissance Woman." She spoke many languages and studied math and science.

The **Scientific Revolution** began during the Renaissance. This was a time of many inventions and discoveries. Scientists showed that it was important to experiment and to watch things closely. Important facts were learned about the sun, the earth, and the planets. People learned more about medicine and how the human body works.

Books were important during the Renaissance. In China, people had been printing books for hundreds of years. In Europe before the Renaissance, books were still being written by hand. There were few

Johannes Gutenberg was able to print books very quickly with his movable type invention.

William Shakespeare

Many of Shakespeare's plays were performed in this theater.

books in Europe. People in Europe then learned to print books using woodblock printing.

A man named Johannes Gutenberg changed the way books were made in Europe. About the year 1450, Gutenberg began to use **movable type** to print books. Movable type was a faster, easier way to make books. People no longer had to carve out each letter. By 1500 there were millions of books in Europe. People started new libraries. Many people learned new ideas by reading books. Many Christians who could read were now able to have their own Bibles at home.

William Shakespeare was an important writer during the English Renaissance. He wrote many wonderful plays. Some plays were very funny, and some were very sad. Shakespeare's plays are about 400 years old. They are part of the world's great literature.

The Renaissance brought lasting changes to Europe. Science and learning became more important. New ideas about art and literature were spread across Europe. Art, music, and plays were created that are still enjoyed today.

Changes in religion also took place during the Renaissance. Why was religion changing? Read the next chapter to find the answer.

Queen Elizabeth I (1533–1603)

Elizabeth I was the daughter of King Henry VIII of England and his second wife, Anne Boleyn. Elizabeth was born in England in 1533. As a child she learned to be a gifted speaker, artist, and musician. In 1558, a few years after King Henry VIII died, Elizabeth I became queen of England. She never married. She ruled as England's monarch until her death in 1603.

Elizabeth made many changes in England during her rule. She made the Church of England the main church of the nation. Queen Elizabeth also worked to end money problems in England. She did this by building up England's trade with other countries. She also ended an expensive war with France.

Queen Elizabeth encouraged people to explore other parts of the world for England. People from England went to North America to set up colonies. An English trade company set up trade between England and parts of Asia, including India. England grew rich through trade.

Queen Elizabeth I

Queen Elizabeth also helped England build a powerful navy. During Queen Elizabeth's rule, England's navy defeated the strong Spanish navy. The strong English navy helped the nation become a leading world power.

Elizabeth encouraged the growth of ideas during the Renaissance. During her rule, new music and works of art were created. Important literature was written. William Shakespeare wrote his poems and plays during this time.

Queen Elizabeth helped England gain wealth, power, and culture. Her rule has been called the Golden Age of England.

Using Vocabulary

Match Up   Finish the sentences in Group A with words from Group B. Write the letter of each correct answer on the blank line.

Group A

1. Religion was very important before the Renaissance, so most artists painted only _____ pictures.

2. *Renaissance* means "_____," or "to be born again."

3. Books, plays, and other written works are all types of _____.

4. The _____ was a time of many discoveries and inventions.

Group B

a. rebirth

b. Scientific Revolution

c. literature

d. religious

Read and Remember

Finish the Sentence   Draw a circle around the word or words that best complete each sentence.

1. The pictures painted by _____ told about stories from the Bible.

   Mona Lisa   Michelangelo   Tarquinia Molza

2. The Renaissance began in _____.

   England   France   Italy

3. _____ used movable type to print books during the Renaissance.

   Leonardo da Vinci   Johannes Gutenberg   Michelangelo

4. William Shakespeare wrote some of the world's best _____.

   literature   Bible stories   science experiments

5. Queen Elizabeth helped end England's money problems by encouraging _____.

   religion   trade   wars

Journal Writing

Write a paragraph that explains how Europe changed during the Renaissance. Tell at least three ways that Europe changed.

Skill Builder

Reading a Flow Chart   A **flow chart** is a chart that shows you facts in the correct order they occur. This flow chart shows how a book is **bound**, or put together. Read the chart. Then circle the words that complete the sentences.

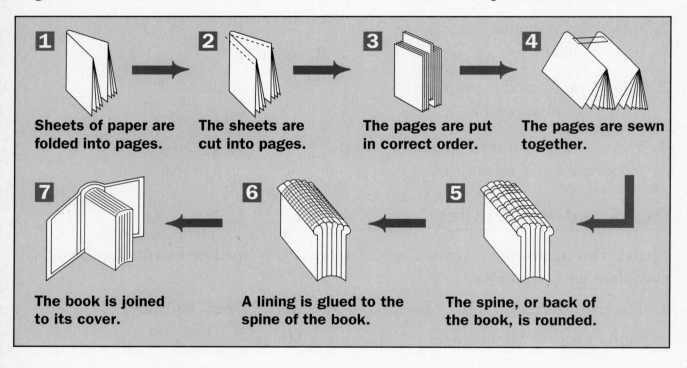

1 Sheets of paper are folded into pages.

2 The sheets are cut into pages.

3 The pages are put in correct order.

4 The pages are sewn together.

7 The book is joined to its cover.

6 A lining is glued to the spine of the book.

5 The spine, or back of the book, is rounded.

1. In the first step, the sheets of paper are _____ into pages.

 sewn   torn   folded

2. After the pages are put in the correct order, they are _____ .

 glued to the cover   sewn together   cut in half

3. In step 5 the spine of the book is _____ .

 rounded   flattened   glued

4. In the last step, the book is joined to its _____ .

 lining   cover   needle

CHAPTER 17

The Reformation

The Roman Catholic Church was rich and powerful during the Middle Ages. In western Europe all Christians belonged to the Roman Catholic Church. About the year 1500, some Catholics wanted to make changes in the Church. These people started the **Reformation**.

The Reformation was a movement to change the Roman Catholic Church. People tried to change some teachings and practices of the Church.

Why did some Catholics work to make changes in the Church? They thought that the pope and the Catholic Church had too much power, land, and wealth. They thought that the leaders of the Catholic Church were **abusing** their power. Peasants, nobles, and kings had to obey the pope and pay taxes to the Church. Much of the tax money was sent to the pope in Rome. Some Catholics were unhappy because

THINK ABOUT AS YOU READ

1. **Why did some people want to make changes in the Roman Catholic Church?**
2. **How was the Protestant church different from the Roman Catholic Church?**
3. **Why did the Catholic Church start the Counter-Reformation?**

NEW WORDS

♦ **Reformation**
♦ **abusing**
♦ **indulgences**
♦ **forgiven**
♦ **95 Theses**
♦ **divorce**
♦ **Counter-Reformation**

PEOPLE & PLACES

♦ **Martin Luther**
♦ **Germany**
♦ **Pope Leo X**
♦ **Protestants**
♦ **Queen Catherine**
♦ **Jesuits**

Martin Luther nailed to a church door a list called the 95 Theses. This list told about the bad practices of the Church.

they had to pay taxes to the Church in Rome. Others felt that the leaders of the Church no longer cared about religion.

Many Catholics were also unhappy because the Church was selling **indulgences**. An indulgence was a paper that said a person's sins were **forgiven**. People thought these indulgences would help them go to heaven when they died. At first, a person had to earn an indulgence by praying and by doing good work. Later, anyone could buy an indulgence. Some priests sold indulgences so that they could earn money for themselves. Many people thought that the Church should not sell indulgences.

Martin Luther was a Catholic priest in Germany. In 1517 he wrote a list of statements about the bad practices of the Church. This list was called the **95 Theses**. Luther's list told people that it was wrong for the Church to sell indulgences. Luther nailed the 95 Theses to the doors of a church in Germany. Martin Luther became a leader of the Reformation. He did not want to leave the Catholic Church. Instead, he hoped to change the Church.

Martin Luther wanted everyone to read the Bible. He said that the Bible told people how to be good Christians. Luther said that people did not need a pope to tell them what the Bible said or how to be good Christians.

The pope and other Church leaders told Martin Luther to stop speaking out against the Catholic Church. But Luther would not stop spreading his ideas. So in 1520 Pope Leo X told Luther that he could no longer be a member of the Catholic Church.

Many people listened to Martin Luther's ideas. They started new churches. These Christians were no longer Catholics. They were called Protestants. Many Protestant churches were built in Europe. Today there are millions of Protestants around the world.

People in England also did not want to pay taxes to the Catholic Church. The Church held much land

Martin Luther

Pope Leo X

Queen Catherine

King Henry VIII

Anne Boleyn

and power in England. England's king did not want to obey a pope in Rome.

King Henry VIII of England worked against the Catholic Church. Henry was a Catholic. He was married to Queen Catherine. Henry wanted to marry Anne Boleyn. Henry asked the pope to end his marriage to Catherine. But the pope said no. The pope was very powerful.

Henry was angry. Henry and Parliament made two new laws. In 1529 a law was passed that said that the pope had no power in England. In 1534 another law said that the king, not the pope, was the leader of the Church of England. King Henry VIII became the leader of the Church of England. He became a Protestant. The Church of England became a Protestant church. The Catholic Church and the pope had lost power in England. Henry got a **divorce** from Queen Catherine. He married Anne Boleyn. Their daughter, Elizabeth, would one day become one of England's greatest queens. You read about Queen Elizabeth in Chapter 16.

The pope and the other leaders of the Catholic Church did not want people to become Protestants. They wanted people to stay or to become Catholics. The pope and the other leaders of the Church started the **Counter-Reformation**. This was a time when the Catholic Church made changes. The Church

This Protestant minister was one of the important leaders of the Reformation. Here he is speaking to a group of nobles.

Jesuit priest

Page from the Gutenberg bible

stopped selling indulgences. More Catholic priests began to travel across Europe to teach people how to be Catholics. These priests were called Jesuits. They started many schools in Europe. The Jesuits taught many people about the Catholic religion.

After the Reformation, religious wars began in Europe. Catholics believed their religion was the only true religion. They wanted all people to be Catholics. Protestants believed their religion was the only true religion. They wanted all people to be Protestants. All over Europe, Protestants and Catholics fought about religion. They would continue to fight for hundreds of years.

The Reformation brought many changes to Europe. During the Middle Ages, few people knew how to read. Protestants believed that everyone should be able to read the Bible. Many new schools were started. Many people learned to read and write. The Roman Catholic Church was no longer the only church in western Europe. Europe now had many Protestant churches. The pope had less power. The monarchs of Europe had become more powerful. The Reformation caused many changes that can still be felt today.

Using Vocabulary

Find the Meaning   Write on the blank the word or words that best complete each sentence.

1. The **Reformation** was a movement to change the _____.

   Roman Catholic Church   Crusades   Renaissance

2. An **indulgence** said that a person's sins were _____.

   good   bad   forgiven

3. The **95 Theses** was a list that told people that it was wrong for the Roman

   Catholic Church to sell _____.

   indulgences   Bibles   goods

4. A **divorce** allowed Henry VIII to end his _____.

   marriage   taxes   Church of England

Read and Remember

Choose the Answer   Draw a circle around the correct answer.

1. Who told Martin Luther he could no longer be a member of the Church?

   Pope Leo X   Henry VIII   God

2. What did Martin Luther want people to read?

   the Koran   the Bible   Greek plays

3. Who did Henry VIII's law of 1529 say had no power in England?

   the pope   the queen   the middle class

4. Who traveled across Europe to teach people about being Catholics?

   Protestants   Anne Boleyn   Jesuits

5. Which group became more powerful in Europe after the Reformation?

   monarchs   popes   Catholic priests

Finish the Paragraph   Use the words in dark print to finish the paragraph below. Write on the correct blank lines the words you choose.

Protestants   taxes   abusing   indulgences   Martin Luther

_____ wrote the 95 Theses about the bad practices of the Roman Catholic Church. He believed that the pope and other Church leaders were _____ their power. Many Catholics did not like paying _____ to the Church in Rome. They also believed that the Church should not sell _____. For these reasons many Catholics chose to become _____ during the Reformation.

Journal Writing

Both Martin Luther and King Henry VIII were unhappy with the Catholic Church. Write a few sentences that tell why each was unhappy with the Church.

Think and Apply

Cause and Effect   Match each cause on the left with an effect on the right. Write the letter of the effect on the correct blank.

Cause

1. Catholics wanted to go to heaven when they died, so _____

2. The pope would not allow King Henry VIII to divorce Catherine, so _____

3. The Church did not want Catholics to become Protestants, so _____

4. Both Catholics and Protestants believed that their religion was the only true religion, so _____

Effect

a. Henry VIII made the Church of England a Protestant church.

b. it started the Counter-Reformation.

c. they fought religious wars.

d. they bought indulgences.

CHAPTER 18

Explorers Find New Lands

THINK ABOUT AS YOU READ

1. **Why did some people become explorers during the Renaissance?**
2. **Who were some explorers, and what did they find?**
3. **What did the world learn from the explorers?**

NEW WORDS

♦ exploration
♦ compass
♦ voyage
♦ New World

PEOPLE & PLACES

♦ **Vasco da Gama**
♦ **Portugal**
♦ **Christopher Columbus**
♦ **American Indians**
♦ **Ferdinand Magellan**
♦ **Jacques Cartier**
♦ **St. Lawrence River**
♦ **Canada**
♦ **John Cabot**

Would you have wanted to sail across the ocean in the year 1500? You would have sailed slowly in a small ship. Your ship might have been destroyed by strong winds. You might have gotten lost and never returned home. Hundreds of years ago, many explorers bravely sailed across oceans to look for new lands.

Exploration was very important during the Renaissance. Inventions, such as better ships and an improved **compass**, made it easier to explore other lands. The explorations of the Renaissance were the beginning of a time period known as the Age of Exploration.

There were many reasons why people became explorers. Some people became explorers because of trade. They wanted to bring silks and spices from Asia back to Europe. But the land routes to Asia were difficult. Also, merchants that traded goods

On his voyage around Africa to India, Vasco da Gama visited this African king.

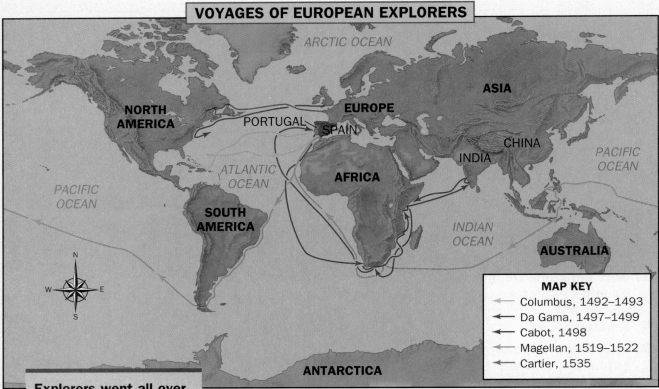

VOYAGES OF EUROPEAN EXPLORERS

ARCTIC OCEAN

NORTH AMERICA

ASIA

EUROPE

PORTUGAL
SPAIN

CHINA

INDIA

PACIFIC OCEAN

ATLANTIC OCEAN

AFRICA

PACIFIC OCEAN

SOUTH AMERICA

INDIAN OCEAN

AUSTRALIA

N
W E
S

ANTARCTICA

MAP KEY
← Columbus, 1492–1493
← Da Gama, 1497–1499
← Cabot, 1498
← Magellan, 1519–1522
← Cartier, 1535

Explorers went all over the world. Which explorer on the map was the only one to sail on the Pacific Ocean?

Vasco da Gama

along the routes increased the prices. So explorers wanted to find new ways to go to Asia.

Some people became explorers because they wanted to find gold. Other people wanted to spread Christianity to people in far-off lands. Some people became explorers for their kings. Many kings in Europe wanted to rule more land. These kings paid explorers to find new lands for them to rule.

Vasco da Gama was an explorer from Portugal. He wanted to find a new way to go to India. In 1497 he left Portugal with four ships. Vasco da Gama and his crew were the first Europeans to go to Asia by sailing all the way around Africa to India. Find da Gama's route on the map above. Da Gama and his crew bought spices in India and sailed back to Portugal. The **voyage** took two years. Da Gama sold the spices for a lot of money. Soon many ships from Portugal sailed around Africa to trade in India.

Christopher Columbus also wanted to find a way to sail from Europe to Asia. At that time many people believed that the world was flat. But Columbus

Christopher Columbus met American Indians when his three ships landed off the coast of the Americas.

Christopher Columbus

Gold plate from the Americas

believed that the world was round. He thought he could find a shorter way to reach Asia by sailing west across the Atlantic Ocean. King Ferdinand and Queen Isabella of Spain helped Columbus. They gave him three small ships.

In 1492 Columbus sailed across the Atlantic Ocean. The voyage was long and slow. After many weeks Columbus and his crew saw land. They did not know that there was land between Europe and Asia. Columbus thought they had reached India. But they were not in India. They had landed on islands off the coast of the Americas. Columbus and his crew were some of the first people from Europe to see the Americas. Europeans called this land the **New World**.

There were people already living in the New World. Columbus called them Indians because he thought he was in India. Today they are called American Indians, or Native Americans. The American Indians had many different civilizations at the time Columbus and other explorers reached the Americas.

Other explorers from Spain explored the lands in North America and South America. The Spanish explorers looked for gold in the New World. The king

Ferdinand Magellan

Jacques Cartier

John Cabot arriving in North America

of Spain said that most of South America belonged to Spain. He said that part of North America also belonged to Spain.

Ferdinand Magellan was another explorer who tried to go to Asia. He thought he could reach Asia by sailing around South America. In 1519 he sailed west from Spain with five ships. He and his crew sailed around South America to the Pacific Ocean. The voyage was hard, and most of the men died. Magellan died on an island in the Pacific. Only one ship was able to sail west to Africa and return to Spain. The 18 men on the ship had sailed all the way around the world in three years. The voyage proved that the world is round.

The French also wanted to find new ways to reach Asia. Jacques Cartier was a French explorer. He thought he could find a short cut to Asia through North America. He wanted to find a river in North America that would go all the way to Asia.

In 1534 Jacques Cartier sailed from France to North America. Cartier and his crew explored the St. Lawrence River in an area that Cartier called Canada. Cartier claimed land in Canada for France. Cartier explored part of the St. Lawrence River from 1535 to 1536. When the river became very narrow, Cartier knew that it was not a short cut to Asia.

The English also wanted to find a short cut to Asia. In 1497 John Cabot sailed west from England. He explored part of North America. Like Cartier, Cabot did not find a new way to Asia. But the king of England said that all of the land Cabot explored in North America belonged to England.

The world learned many things from the explorers of long ago. The explorers showed that ships could sail around Africa to reach Asia. Explorers proved that the world was round and not flat. The Europeans learned about other lands and civilizations. In the next chapter, you will learn about some of the different civilizations in Africa and the Americas.

Using Vocabulary

Analogies   Use the words in dark print to best complete the sentences.

compass   voyage   New World   exploration

1. Marco Polo is to China as Christopher Columbus is to the

_____ .

2. Artist is to paintbrush as sailor is to _____ .

3. Invent is to invention as explore is to _____ .

4. Battle is to fight as journey is to _____ .

Read and Remember

Find the Answer   Put a check (✔) next to each sentence that tells
something true about why people in Europe became explorers. You should
check four sentences.

_____ **1.** Europeans wanted to find a shorter route to Asia.

_____ **2.** People in Europe wanted to see Martin Luther.

_____ **3.** People wanted to find gold.

_____ **4.** People wanted to spread Christianity to other lands.

_____ **5.** People wanted to live in England.

_____ **6.** People wanted to live on manors.

_____ **7.** People wanted to help their kings rule more land.

Journal Writing

There were many explorers during the Age of Exploration. Pick one of the
five explorers mentioned in this chapter. Write a few sentences that explain
why this explorer was important.

Think and Apply

Sequencing Events   Write the numbers **1, 2, 3, 4,** and **5** next to these sentences to show the correct order.

_____   Vasco da Gama left Portugal in 1497 and sailed around Africa to India.

_____   Ferdinand Magellan set sail in 1519 on the voyage that proved the world is round.

_____   Jacques Cartier claimed new land in Canada for France in 1534.

_____   In 1492 Columbus sailed across the Atlantic Ocean to find a shorter way to Asia.

_____   Magellan's crew returned to Spain after three years of sailing all around the world.

Skill Builder

Reading a Historical Map   A **historical map** shows information about events and places during a certain time period. The historical map on page 118 shows the routes of some explorers in the 1400s and 1500s. Study the map. Then write the answer to each question below.

1. When was da Gama's voyage? _____

2. What color is used on the map to show Columbus' route? _____

3. Which three explorers sailed only in the Atlantic Ocean? _____

_____

4. What land did da Gama sail around? _____

5. Which explorer sailed around South America? _____

6. Who sailed farthest south? _____

7. Which explorer sailed down the east coast of North America in 1498?

_____

Skill Builder

Reading a Double Bar Graph

A **double bar graph** compares facts by using two different colored bars. This double bar graph shows how much gold and silver was shipped to Spain from the Americas from 1531 to 1560. The blue bar shows how much gold was shipped to Spain. The green bar shows how much silver was shipped to Spain. Study the bar graph. Then draw a circle around the numbers, dates, or words that best complete the sentences below.

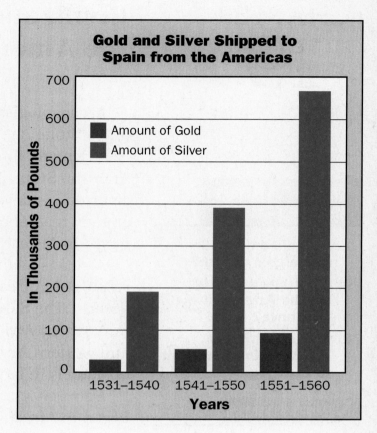

Gold and Silver Shipped to Spain from the Americas

1. The bar graph shows that more _____ was shipped to Spain from the Americas from 1531 to 1560.

   gold   silver   copper

2. The largest amount of gold was shipped to Spain during the years _____.

   1531–1540   1541–1550   1551–1560

3. During the years 1531–1540, Spain received about _____ pounds of silver.

   100 thousand   200 thousand   400 thousand

4. The amounts of both gold and silver being shipped to Spain _____ from 1531 to 1560.

   increased   decreased   stayed about the same

5. Spain received about _____ pounds more silver in 1541–1550 than in 1531–1540.

   100 thousand   200 thousand   400 thousand

Civilizations in Africa and the Americas

1. **How did empires in Africa gain wealth?**
2. **What kinds of skills did the Aztec and the Inca have?**
3. **How did different American Indians adapt to their regions?**

NEW WORDS

♦ **caravans**
♦ **sacrifice**
♦ **regions**
♦ **adapted**
♦ **adobe**

PEOPLE & PLACES

♦ **Sahara**
♦ **Ghana**
♦ **Mali Empire**
♦ **Zimbabwe**
♦ **Monomutapa Empire**
♦ **Mexico**
♦ **Aztec**
♦ **Inca**
♦ **Andes Mountains**
♦ **Algonquin**
♦ **Hopi**
♦ **Mansa Musa**
♦ **Timbuktu**

Archaeologists have found many Stone Age bones and tools in Africa and in the Americas. After the Stone Age, many civilizations developed on these continents. You have already read about the great civilization of ancient Egypt in Africa.

Africa is a land of gold and many other natural resources. Africa also has forests, meadows, and deserts. The Sahara is the world's largest desert. It is in northern Africa. To trade gold and salt in northern and western Africa, many people crossed the Sahara on camels in large **caravans**.

Between A.D. 300 and 1600, great trading empires began in Africa. Some of these empires developed in western Africa, just south of the Sahara. One trading empire in western Africa was Ghana. It developed in the 300s. The rulers of Ghana taxed the goods that passed through the empire. The Ghana Empire became wealthy from these taxes.

These buildings of the city of Zimbabwe were first built in Africa around A.D. 1000.

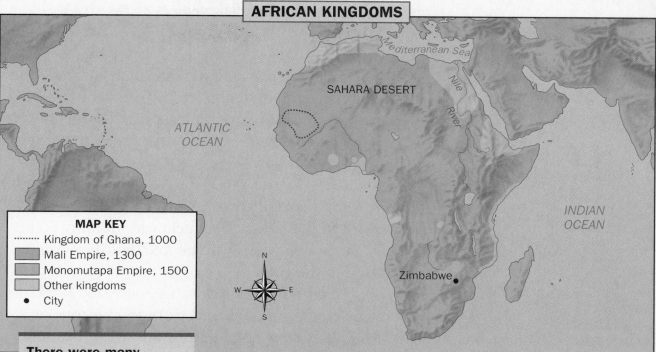

AFRICAN KINGDOMS

SAHARA DESERT

Mediterranean Sea

Nile River

ATLANTIC OCEAN

INDIAN OCEAN

Zimbabwe

MAP KEY
- ·········· Kingdom of Ghana, 1000
- Mali Empire, 1300
- Monomutapa Empire, 1500
- Other kingdoms
- ● City

N W E S

There were many African civilizations all over the continent. What was one empire near the Indian Ocean?

African woman at a market

The people of Ghana were among the first in Africa to use iron to make tools and weapons. These strong weapons helped the people of Ghana conquer other groups of people. By the year 1000, Ghana was a very strong empire. But soon other people conquered Ghana. During the 1200s Ghana became part of the Mali Empire.

Other empires began in southeastern Africa. The city of Zimbabwe was built around A.D. 1000. The word *zimbabwe* means "house of stone." During the 1400s Zimbabwe became part of a rich and powerful empire. This empire was the Monomutapa Empire. The empire gained most of its wealth from the mining and trading of gold. Like Ghana, the Monomutapa Empire taxed all the goods that passed through its lands. Many stone buildings from the Monomutapa Empire have been found in the modern country of Zimbabwe.

Many of the customs from these and other African civilizations are still followed today. Many people in Africa make items that other Africans made hundreds of years ago. One such item is jewelry. Some people also wear clothing that is like the clothing worn in Africa long ago. Customs are very important all over Africa.

While civilizations were developing in Africa, other civilizations were beginning in the Americas. Two of the most advanced American Indian civilizations were in Mexico and in South America. One was the Aztec. The Aztec civilization began in Mexico around the year A.D. 1200. By the 1400s the Aztec had a wealthy empire with a strong government. Religion was very important to the Aztec. They believed in many gods. They went to war to capture people that they could **sacrifice** to the gods.

The Aztec had many skills. They created land for farms by digging up mud from the bottom of a nearby lake. They used the mud to form islands. They grew crops such as corn on the islands. The Aztec also developed a written language in which pictures stood for ideas. They invented a calendar. They made works of art out of gold and stones. Many Aztec foods such as chocolate and tacos are still enjoyed today.

Aztec calendar stone

CIVILIZATIONS IN AFRICA AND THE AMERICAS

Civilization	Location	Dates	Interesting Facts
Ghana	West Africa	about A.D. 300–1076	Made iron weapons. Controlled caravan routes through the Sahara.
Monomutapa	Southeast Africa	about 1450– early 1500s	Made buildings using stones without clay.
Aztec	Mexico in North America	about 1200–1521	Developed written language and calendar. Sacrificed people to the gods.
Inca	Andes Mountains in South America	about 1200–1532	Built roads and bridges. Built large temples.
Algonquin	Eastern Woodlands region of North America	?–present	Used wood and animal skins to build homes. Used canoes, snowshoes, and sleds for travel.
Hopi	Southwest region of North America	?–present	Grew cotton and wove it into cloth. Built homes with adobe.

The Inca built their cities in the tall mountains of the Andes.

American Indians, 1500

American Indians adapted to their regions.

The Inca in South America were developing their own empire at about the same time as were the Aztec. Their civilization began around 1200 in the Andes Mountains of South America. They made their civilization larger by conquering nearby groups of people. By the 1400s the Inca had formed an empire.

Religion was an important part of the Inca way of life. The Inca believed in many gods. The Inca also made beautiful cloth and works of art. They irrigated their farms. They did not have a system of writing.

The Inca were known for their building skills. They built many temples and government buildings. They built thousands of miles of roads. They also built bridges that went across rivers and between mountains to connect roads.

Many American Indian groups lived in different **regions** of North America. Each group **adapted** to the different resources and climates of the regions where they lived. Different groups within the same region often developed similar cultures. The map on this page shows some of the different regions in North America.

One group of American Indians who lived in the Eastern Woodlands region was the Algonquin. Many Algonquin also lived in the southeast part of

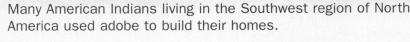

Many American Indians living in the Southwest region of North America used adobe to build their homes.

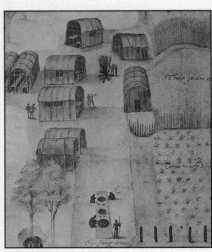

Algonquin village

Hopi today

Canada. There are many forests, lakes, and rivers in the areas where they lived. The Algonquin fished and hunted to get food. They also gathered berries and wild plants for food. They used animal skins for their clothes and homes. The Algonquin also used wood from trees to make their homes. They had their own religion. There are still Algonquin living in North America today.

The Hopi were a peaceful group of American Indians who lived in the Southwest. Religion was very important to the Hopi. The climate where the Hopi lived is hot and dry. Few plants and animals live there. However, there are some large rivers in the Southwest. The Hopi hunted animals and gathered nuts and seeds. They also used river water to grow crops. They grew cotton to make their clothing. There is little wood in the Southwest. So the Hopi used **adobe** to make their houses. Adobe is a mixture of desert clay and straw. Today many Hopi still live in the Southwest.

What happened to the civilizations in Africa and the Americas after Europeans arrived? The next chapter provides the answer to this question.

Mansa Musa (1297?–1332)

The Mali Empire began in western Africa during the early 1200s. Ghana became part of the Mali Empire. Mali was a strong, large empire. It gained much wealth by controlling the gold and salt trade. Mali became a center of trade.

In 1307 Mansa Musa became king of Mali. He was a great ruler. Mansa Musa made the Mali Empire a center of culture in western Africa. He also made the Mali Empire much larger. He did this by conquering people in nearby lands. Mansa Musa also used peaceful ways to gain more land.

Mansa Musa was a Muslim. He spread Islam throughout the empire. He had mosques built in many cities in the empire. Like all Muslims he was required to visit Mecca. So in 1324 Mansa Musa began a pilgrimage to Mecca. It took him more than a year to travel the 3,500 miles. Thousands of his people went with him. Hundreds of camels carried gold. Mansa Musa gave away gold to poor people he met on his pilgrimage.

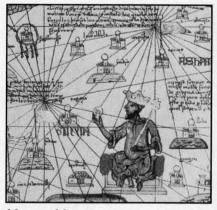

Mansa Musa

Mansa Musa brought back to Mali teachers and builders he met on his pilgrimage. He had the builders construct a school in the Mali city of Timbuktu. Timbuktu became a great center of learning. People in Timbuktu could study Islam and law. Timbuktu also became a center of trade.

Mansa Musa ruled Mali until 1332. During his rule, Mali was a large and powerful empire. The rulers who came after Mansa Musa were weak. They could not control the large empire. About one hundred years after Mansa Musa's death, Mali was conquered by people in another empire. The great Mali empire came to an end.

Using Vocabulary

Finish Up   Choose the words in dark print to best complete the sentences. Write the words on the correct blank lines.

sacrifice   caravans   adobe   regions   adapted

1. Many _____ of people and animals crossed the Sahara to trade in northern Africa.

2. The Hopi _____ to the resources in their area by using river water to grow crops in the hot, dry climate.

3. Different _____ of a continent often also have different natural resources and climates.

4. The Aztec sometimes killed people because the Aztec believed they should _____ people to the gods.

5. The Hopi used _____, a mixture of desert clay and straw, to build their houses.

Read and Remember

Finish the Sentence   Draw a circle around the word or words that best complete each sentence.

1. The _____ Empire became wealthy from the taxes on goods that passed through the empire.

   Aztec   Ghana   Inca

2. The Monomutapa Empire included the great city of _____.

   Zimbabwe   Sahara   Timbuktu

3. The _____ are known for building bridges that reached across rivers and between mountains.

   Monomutapa   Aztec   Inca

4. The Algonquin Indians lived in the _____ region.

    Southwest   Plains   Eastern Woodlands

5. Mansa Musa made a pilgrimage to Mecca from the _____ Empire.

    Ghana   Inca   Mali

Think and Apply

Distinguishing Relevant Information   Imagine that you want to explain to a friend about life in early civilizations in Africa and the Americas. Read each sentence below. Decide which sentences are relevant to what you will say. Put a check (✔) next to the relevant sentences. There are four relevant sentences.

_____ **1.** Religion was an important part of many civilizations in Africa and the Americas.

_____ **2.** The Sahara is the world's largest desert.

_____ **3.** The people of Ghana used iron to make their tools and weapons.

_____ **4.** People could go to school in Timbuktu.

_____ **5.** The Aztec made works of art out of gold and stones.

_____ **6.** Many Hopi and Algonquin live in North America today.

Skill Builder

Reading a Chart   Read the chart on page 126 about civilizations in Africa and the Americas. Then write the answer to each question below.

1. What is one interesting fact about the Ghana Empire? _____

_____

2. Where was the Monomutapa Empire located? _____

3. When did the Aztec civilization exist? _____

4. Which civilization lived in the Southwest region? _____

5. Which civilization sometimes had snow? _____

Colonies for Europe

THINK ABOUT AS YOU READ

1. **Why did countries in Europe want to rule colonies?**
2. **How did ruling countries hurt their colonies?**
3. **What was the French and Indian War?**

NEW WORDS

- ♦ **ruling countries**
- ♦ **raw materials**
- ♦ **plantations**
- ♦ **trading posts**
- ♦ **freedom of religion**

PEOPLE & PLACES

- ♦ **Brazil**
- ♦ **Quebec**
- ♦ **Mississippi River**
- ♦ **Pilgrims**
- ♦ **Great Britain**
- ♦ **British**

As you read in Chapter 18, European explorers traveled to many far-off lands. European countries began to start colonies in Africa and the Americas. They also built up trade with India and China. The map on page 134 shows the American lands ruled by European countries.

Why did European countries want to rule colonies in the Americas? One reason was that the **ruling countries** wanted to find gold and silver in their colonies. Another reason was that colonies helped trade. They were good places for merchants to sell their goods. A third reason was that colonies gave the ruling countries **raw materials** that they did not have at home. Metals, cotton, and wood were important raw materials from the colonies. Colonies sent goods like coffee, sugar, and chocolate to their ruling countries. A fourth reason was that ruling countries also wanted to spread Christianity to the American Indians.

European countries started colonies in the Americas.

Spain, Portugal, and England brought people from Africa to work as slaves in the colonies.

In many ways the ruling countries hurt their colonies. Colonies were only allowed to trade with their ruling country. Colonies were not allowed to make many things they needed. The colonies needed cloth, guns, and tools. They had to buy these things from the ruling countries. The ruling countries became richer from this trade.

There were other ways that ruling countries hurt their colonies. The ruling countries wanted the people in the colonies to work for them. But the countries did not want to pay workers much money. Ruling countries wanted slaves to work in their colonies in mines and on large farms called **plantations**. Spain and Portugal forced American Indians to work as slaves. Spain, Portugal, and England also brought people from Africa to work as slaves in the colonies.

An American Indian dying from a European disease

As more Europeans came to America, thousands of American Indians died. Many died from the hard, dangerous work they were forced to do as slaves. But even more died as a result of disease. Many Europeans brought diseases that had never before been in the Americas. Sometimes diseases killed entire groups of American Indians. Then the cultures of these American Indians were also destroyed.

Spanish soldiers conquered the Aztec in 1521.

Colonies in the Americas, 1700

MAP KEY
- British
- French
- Spanish
- Portuguese
- Other

Which European countries had colonies? Portugal had **trading posts** in India and China. It ruled colonies in Africa. In South America, Portugal also ruled a large colony called Brazil.

Spain also built a large empire. Spanish soldiers conquered the Aztec and Inca empires. Spain also conquered other lands in North America and in South America. Many Spanish colonies began. People in the Spanish colonies sent gold and silver to Spain.

France ruled colonies in North America. The French ruled Quebec and most of eastern Canada. They ruled land around the Mississippi River in North America.

The French came to North America to trade. The American Indians hunted many animals for their furs. The French traded with the American Indians for furs. In France the French sold these furs for a lot of money.

English people came to live in North America beginning in 1607. Some English people came to North America to find gold. Other English people came to North America because they wanted **freedom of religion**. Freedom of religion means that people can belong to any religious group they choose. Everyone in England had to belong to the Church of England. Many English people did not

The French traded with the American Indians for fur.

Many American Indians helped the French fight the British during the French and Indian War.

Pilgrims landing in North America

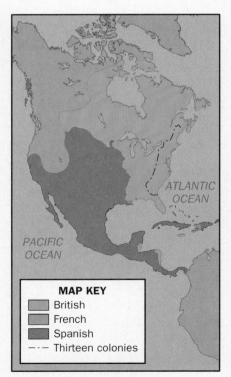
ATLANTIC OCEAN

PACIFIC OCEAN

MAP KEY
- British
- French
- Spanish
- –·– Thirteen colonies

North America in 1763

like the Church of England. Some of these people were called the Pilgrims. In 1620 the Pilgrims moved to North America. There they had religious freedom.

In 1707 England joined with two smaller nations to become part of a larger nation called Great Britain. The people of Great Britain became known as the British. The colonies of England were now called British colonies.

Great Britain did not want France to rule any colonies in North America. France did not want Great Britain to have colonies in North America. In 1754 the French and the British fought over who would rule North America. Their fight was called the French and Indian War. Many American Indians helped the French fight the British. The British army was stronger. In 1763 Great Britain won the war. France lost its colonies in North America. Now Great Britain and Spain ruled most of North America.

Great Britain ruled 13 colonies in America. But soon the people in these colonies decided they did not want to be ruled by Great Britain. You will learn about the American fight for freedom in Chapter 21.

Using Vocabulary

Finish the Paragraph   Use the words in dark print to finish the paragraph below. Write on the correct blank lines the words you choose.

ruling countries   diseases   plantations   freedom of religion

Some Europeans came to the Americas because they were sent by their

_____ to start colonies. Some English people who did not want

to belong to the Church of England came to the Americas because they wanted

_____ . But the colonies hurt many American Indians and

Africans. Many were forced to work as slaves on large farms called

_____ . Many American Indians became sick and died from

European _____ .

Read and Remember

Write the Answer   Write one or more sentences to answer each question.

1. Which ruling countries had both American Indians and African slaves in

the colonies? _____

_____

2. Which empires did the Spanish soldiers conquer in the Americas? _____

_____

3. When did England become a part of Great Britain? _____

_____

4. How did France lose its colonies in North America? _____

_____

_____

Think and Apply

Exclusions   One word or phrase in each group does not belong. Find that word or phrase and cross it out. Then write on a separate sheet of paper a sentence that tells how the other words are alike.

1. Portugal
Spain
Brazil
France

2. find gold
increase trade
spread Christianity
get sick from diseases

3. coffee
sugar
land
chocolate

4. destroyed the Aztec Empire
settled in Quebec
traded for furs
went to war against Great Britain

Skill Builder

Reading a Circle Graph   A **circle graph** shows how all of something is divided into parts. Most often a circle graph shows **percent,** or parts per one hundred. This circle graph shows how the population of the world in 1650 was divided among the continents. Study the circle graph. Then draw a circle around each correct answer below.

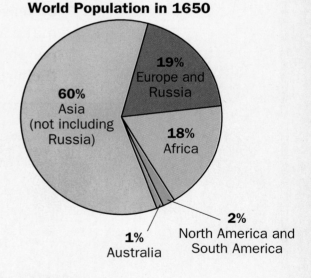

World Population in 1650

60% Asia (not including Russia)

19% Europe and Russia

18% Africa

1% Australia

2% North America and South America

1. Which continent had the largest population in 1650?

Europe   Asia   Africa

2. Which continent had about 1% of the world population in 1650?

Antarctica   Australia   Africa

3. Which continent had about the same percent of the world population as Europe and Russia?

North America   Asia   Africa

Unit 4   Revolutions

People were angry and unhappy. They did not like their rulers or the laws of their government. They decided to fight for their freedom. Their wars were called revolutions.

Many nations had revolutions between 1775 and 1850. Freedom became an important idea. The fight for freedom began with the 13 British colonies in America. Other nations joined the fight for freedom. Their revolutions changed the world.

What caused these revolutions? For hundreds of years, most monarchs had full power to make all laws. Things began to change. Many people did not want powerful monarchs to be their rulers. People in colonies did not want to be ruled by other countries. People wanted laws that would be fair to the rich and to the poor. They wanted the freedom to make laws for their nations. They wanted to vote for their leaders. People in many lands fought for these ideas.

You will be reading about important revolutions that happened between 1775 and 1850. How did the fight for freedom begin in the 13 American colonies? Why did the people of France fight against their king? How did countries in Latin America win their freedom? As you read Unit 4, think about how different

the world would be if people had not fought in revolutions. Think about why people feel that freedom is worth fighting for.

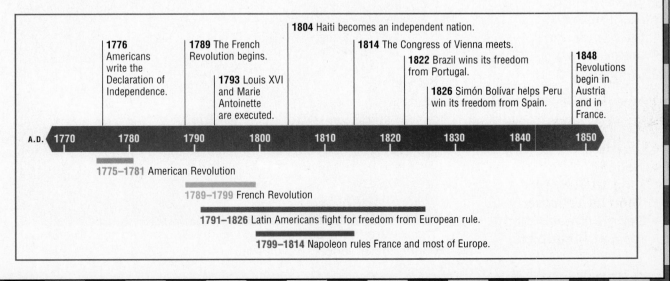

1804 Haiti becomes an independent nation.

1776 Americans write the Declaration of Independence.

1789 The French Revolution begins.

1793 Louis XVI and Marie Antoinette are executed.

1814 The Congress of Vienna meets.

1822 Brazil wins its freedom from Portugal.

1826 Simón Bolívar helps Peru win its freedom from Spain.

1848 Revolutions begin in Austria and in France.

A.D. 1770 1780 1790 1800 1810 1820 1830 1840 1850

1775–1781 American Revolution

1789–1799 French Revolution

1791–1826 Latin Americans fight for freedom from European rule.

1799–1814 Napoleon rules France and most of Europe.

CHAPTER 21

The American Revolution

Many people from countries in Europe came to live in America. They came from such countries as Great Britain, France, Germany, Sweden, and Holland. People came to America for many reasons. Some people came because they wanted freedom of religion. Some people came to own land and become rich. Some British people came to America because they did not like the king or the laws of Great Britain.

Great Britain started 13 American colonies along the Atlantic Ocean. The colonies belonged to Great Britain. Americans had to obey the laws and the king of Great Britain.

You read in Chapter 20 that Great Britain and France fought a war about which nation would rule in America. Great Britain spent a lot of money fighting for America in the French and Indian War. Great Britain wanted the American **colonists** to help

There were many battles between the British and the Americans during the American Revolution.

Americans became angry when King George III passed new tax laws.

King George III

British tax stamp

pay for the war. So in 1764 Parliament and the king of Great Britain, George III, passed a tax law called the **Sugar Act**. The Sugar Act said that Americans had to pay taxes for certain goods that were brought to the American colonies. Some of the taxed goods were sugar and coffee.

In 1765 Parliament and King George III passed another tax law for the American colonies. This new law, the **Stamp Act**, said that Americans had to pay taxes on newspapers and other printed items.

The Sugar Act and the Stamp Act made the colonists angry. In Great Britain, voters helped make their tax laws in Parliament. But Americans were not allowed to help Parliament write tax laws for the colonies. King George said that Americans must obey laws that were made for them in Great Britain.

Americans said that it was unfair for the British to write tax laws for the colonies. The colonists wanted to send American **representatives** to Parliament. They wanted the right to help write their own tax laws. People in Great Britain had this right.

King George removed the Stamp Act in 1766. But in 1767 King George and Parliament wrote more tax laws for America. The new laws taxed such things

This battle near Boston in 1775 was one of the major battles of the American Revolution.

Battles of the American Revolution

MAP KEY
✳ Major battle

ATLANTIC OCEAN

Thomas Jefferson

as tea and paper. Americans did not want to obey laws that were made in Great Britain. Some angry Americans decided to fight. They would fight for the right to make their own laws.

In 1775 a war began between Great Britain and America. The war was called the **American Revolution**. British soldiers and American soldiers fought each other in America. At first, Americans fought because they wanted King George to let them write their own laws. But then their goals changed. In 1776 Americans decided that they did not want to be ruled by Great Britain. They wanted America to become an **independent** nation. Americans were fighting for their freedom.

In 1776 Americans decided to tell the world that America was a free country. American leaders asked Thomas Jefferson to write a paper called the **Declaration of Independence**. Jefferson used some of John Locke's ideas about democracy in the Declaration of Independence. This paper told the world that the 13 American colonies had the right to make laws for themselves. It said that the colonies no longer belonged to Great Britain and would no longer obey King George. The Declaration

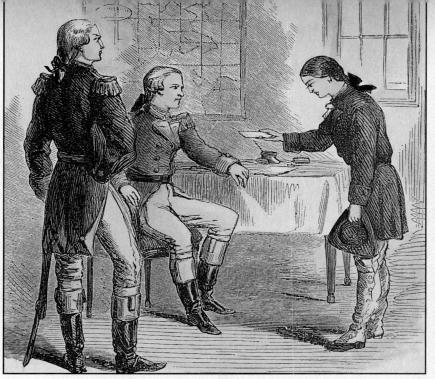

An American woman named Deborah Sampson dressed as a male soldier so that she could fight for her country.

The Declaration of Independence

of Independence told the world that America was an independent country.

The American soldiers fought many battles against the British. General George Washington was the leader of the American army. He had fought in the French and Indian War. Washington was a strong leader. He lost many battles, but he kept on fighting for American freedom.

Many different Americans fought together to win the American Revolution. African Americans and women fought against the British. Protestants, Catholics, and Jews fought together in the war. People from other nations also helped the Americans fight in the war.

In 1781 Americans won the American Revolution. In 1783 Great Britain signed a **peace treaty** that said that Great Britain no longer ruled the American colonies. But Great Britain did not lose all of its land in North America. It still ruled parts of Canada. Americans were free from British rule. However, independence from Great Britain did not mean freedom for African American slaves.

American leaders wrote the United States Constitution in 1787.

The Constitution

President George Washington

The American Revolution brought about many changes in America. The 13 colonies were now 13 states. Americans called their nation the United States of America. The nation needed its own laws and plan of government. In 1787 American leaders wrote laws for their new nation. The leaders also used ideas about law and democracy from people such as John Locke. They also used ideas from the Magna Carta and from Great Britain's Parliament. All these ideas helped the leaders write the **Constitution**.

The Constitution gave the United States a strong government. This government ruled all the states. The laws helped the nation become a democracy. It was also a republic. The new nation would not have a monarch. Americans would choose a President to be their leader. George Washington became the first President of the United States in 1789.

The American Revolution also brought changes to Europe. The people in Europe learned how Americans fought to become an independent nation and a democracy. Soon people in some parts of Europe would also fight for their rights and freedom.

Using Vocabulary

Match Up Finish the sentences in Group A with words from Group B. Write the letter of each correct answer on the blank line.

Group A

1. American colonists had to pay taxes on printed materials after Parliament passed a tax law called the _____ .

2. Americans wanted to be free, or _____ , of British rule.

3. The American colonists fought the _____ so that they could form a new nation.

4. At the end of the war, Great Britain signed a _____ saying that it no longer ruled the 13 colonies.

Group B

a. American Revolution

b. peace treaty

c. independent

d. Stamp Act

Read and Remember

Write the Answer Write one or more sentences to answer each question.

1. Why did the Sugar Act and the Stamp Act make Americans angry? _____

_____

2. What were two things the Declaration of Independence said? _____

_____

3. What was the American government like after the Constitution was written?

_____

4. How did the American Revolution affect Europe? _____

_____

Think and Apply

Cause and Effect　Match each cause on the left with an effect on the right. Write the letter of the effect on the correct blank.

Cause

1. Some British people did not like the laws of Great Britain, so _____

2. Great Britain had spent a lot of money to fight for America in the French and Indian War, so _____

3. Americans were not represented in Parliament, so _____

Effect

a. they thought tax laws written for the colonies were unfair.

b. they came to live in America.

c. Great Britain wanted America to help pay for the war.

Skill Builder

Understanding a Political Cartoon　A **political cartoon** is a drawing that shows what an artist thinks about a certain person, event, or **issue**. An issue is something that people have different opinions about. Sometimes political cartoons seem funny, but they are usually about serious ideas. Benjamin Franklin drew this political cartoon to help unite the American colonies against Great Britain. Study the cartoon. Then answer the questions below.

1. What animal is used to stand for the American colonies?_____

2. What did Franklin believe would happen to the colonies if they did not unite

   against Great Britain?_____

   _____

3. Imagine you were an American colonist. Would Franklin's political cartoon have made you want to help fight the British? Explain your answer on a separate sheet of paper.

Crossword Puzzle

Each sentence below has a word missing. Choose the missing word for each sentence from the words in dark print. Then write the words in the correct places on the puzzle.

_____ **ACROSS** _____

Constitution   Declaration   represented   obey

1. King George said that Americans must _____ laws made for them.

2. The _____ of Independence said that the American colonies did not belong to Great Britain.

3. The laws of the United States were written in the _____.

4. The Americans wanted to be _____ in Parliament.

_____ **DOWN** _____

colonists   ruled   Act   freedom

5. Some people came to America because they wanted _____ of religion.

6. The Sugar _____ taxed such things as sugar and coffee.

7. Angry _____ decided to fight for the right to write their own tax laws.

8. In 1776 Americans decided they did not want to be _____ by the British.

The French Revolution

THINK ABOUT AS YOU READ

1. **Why did the French Revolution begin?**
2. **How did the National Assembly change France's government?**
3. **How did the French Revolution change France?**

NEW WORDS

♦ **French Revolution**
♦ **absolute rule**
♦ **estate**
♦ **National Assembly**
♦ **Bastille**
♦ **"Liberty, Equality, Fraternity"**
♦ **royal**

PEOPLE & PLACES

♦ **King Louis XVI**
♦ **Paris**
♦ **Jacobins**
♦ **Marie Antoinette**
♦ **Napoleon Bonaparte**
♦ **Austria**

Imagine a time when the people in France were so angry that they killed their king and queen and thousands of other people. This was the time of the **French Revolution**. It began in 1789. The revolution was a ten-year fight to change old laws and to gain more rights.

Before 1789 the French monarchs had been very powerful. They had **absolute rule**. They made all the laws. People had few rights. The French people learned how Americans had won freedom in the American Revolution. Many French people wanted more freedom, too. They also wanted more rights.

There were three groups of people in France before the French Revolution. Each group was called an **estate**. People who worked for the Roman Catholic Church were in the First Estate. Rich nobles were in the Second Estate. People such as peasants,

In 1789 the French people gained power by capturing a prison called the Bastille.

People in the Third Estate

King Louis XVI

city workers, lawyers, doctors, and merchants were in the Third Estate. Only a very small part of the French population was in the First and Second Estates. Most French people were in the Third Estate.

The people of the First and Second Estates owned much of the land in France. Most were very wealthy. The people in the First and Second Estates did not pay taxes. The Third Estate was forced to pay very high taxes. The people in the Third Estate wanted the other estates to pay taxes. They wanted to change the laws of France.

King Louis XVI was the king of France in 1789. He wanted both the Second and Third Estates to pay taxes because France needed money. The French had spent too much money fighting long wars against other nations. They had fought in the French and Indian War. The French had also spent a lot of money helping Americans fight in their war for freedom.

The people of the Second Estate said they would not pay taxes. Most people in the Third Estate did not have enough money to pay more taxes. The Third Estate felt that the king had too much power and wealth. The Third Estate started the **National Assembly**. They said they spoke for all the people of France. People from the First and Second Estates also met with the National Assembly. The people of the National Assembly told King Louis that they would make new laws for France. They said that absolute rule in France was over. The French Revolution had begun!

King Louis did not want the National Assembly to make new laws. The king called soldiers to Paris, the capital of France. Many French people became very angry. They started many riots in Paris. There was fighting and killing in the city's streets. Fighting also began in other parts of France.

The **Bastille** was an old prison in Paris. For many years French kings had sent many people to the Bastille. On July 14, 1789, angry French people attacked the Bastille. They were looking for guns and other weapons inside. The French people freed the prisoners. The fall of the Bastille meant that King Louis had less power. It also made the National Assembly stronger. July 14 is now a French holiday called Bastille Day. Each year France celebrates its independence on this day.

"Liberty, Equality, Fraternity" became very important words during the revolution. People shouted these words. They carried signs and flags with these words on them. The words meant that all people should have freedom and equal rights.

French soldiers

On August 27, 1789, the National Assembly signed a paper called the Declaration of the Rights of Man and of the Citizen. This important paper said that everyone had freedom and equal rights. It also said that people had freedom of speech and freedom of religion. By 1791 the National Assembly had also written a new constitution. The National Assembly said all laws must be fair to the rich and to the poor. Everyone had to pay taxes and obey the new constitution.

The National Assembly said Louis would still be the king of France. But King Louis lost most of his power. The National Assembly, not the king, would make laws for France.

The National Assembly

King Louis did not want to fight the angry people in France. So he agreed to both the Declaration of the Rights of Man and the new constitution. But then in 1791, King Louis and his family tried to escape from France. Louis wanted rulers from other countries to help him have absolute rule in France again. The **royal** family was captured by French soldiers and put in prison.

In 1792 some French people decided they did not want another king. Like the Americans in the United States, the French started a republic. People called Jacobins became the rulers of the French Republic. The Jacobins then tried to kill everyone who was

The angry people of France rioted outside the palace of King Louis XVI and his family.

Napoleon Bonaparte

against the French Revolution and the new republic. Thousands of French people, including both nobles and peasants, were executed. In 1793 King Louis and his wife, Marie Antoinette, were also executed.

The French hated the Jacobins because they killed so many people. So in 1794 people began to fight the Jacobins. The Jacobins lost power. In 1795 a new group of people became the rulers of the French Republic. They wrote a new constitution. But they could not bring peace to France. Riots continued in the nation's streets.

The French Revolution ended in 1799. It ended when Napoleon Bonaparte became the ruler of France. He started a strong government. He brought peace to France and war to the rest of Europe. You will read about Napoleon in Chapter 23.

Thousands of people died during the long years of the French Revolution. But the revolution also brought some good changes to France. The people of France had more freedom. They all had to pay taxes. They all had equal rights. The old laws of France were gone.

Marie Antoinette (1755–1793)

Marie Antoinette was born to a royal family in the country of Austria in 1755. She married the prince of France when she was just 14 years old. In 1774 her husband became King Louis XVI of France. Marie Antoinette became the queen of France at age 19.

Marie Antoinette was not well liked in France. She was from Austria, an enemy of France. She also did not seem to care that France was having money problems. She did not seem to worry that many people in France were starving. She spent large amounts of France's money on clothes and other items for herself. She also spent money on her friends. This made the French people angry.

As you have read, the French Revolution began in 1789. In October 1789 Marie Antoinette, King Louis XVI, and their children were forced to move to Paris. They were treated like prisoners. Marie asked for help from her brother, the ruler of Austria. She and Louis wanted her brother and other rulers to help them fight for more power. Finally, Marie Antoinette and her family tried to escape from France. The royal family was caught and returned to Paris. The people of France were angry that Marie Antoinette and the king had tried to leave France.

Marie Antoinette continued to try to get help from other European countries. In 1792 she was caught trying to give Austria secret information about the French armies. Marie and her husband were sent to prison. In 1793 the French people used a special machine to chop off the heads of Marie and Louis. Neither Marie nor Louis showed any fear as they were executed.

Marie Antoinette

The palace of Louis XVI and Marie Antoinette

Using Vocabulary

Analogies   Use the words in dark print to best complete the sentences.

Rights of Man   National Assembly   estate   French Revolution

1. The American Revolution was to America as the _____ was to France.

2. A caste was to ancient India as an _____ was to France.

3. The House of Commons was to Great Britain as the _____ was to France.

4. The Declaration of Independence is to the United States as the Declaration of the _____ is to France.

Read and Remember

Finish the Sentence   Draw a circle around the word or words that best complete each sentence.

1. People who worked for the Roman Catholic Church were in the _____ Estate.
   First   Second   Third

2. Rich nobles were in the _____ Estate.
   First   Second   Third

3. The National Assembly made new _____ for France.
   buildings   prisons   laws

4. Marie Antoinette asked for help from her brother, the ruler of _____.
   Spain   Austria   France

5. The Jacobins _____ King Louis and Marie Antoinette.
   saved   liked   executed

6. The French Revolution ended when _____ became the ruler of France.
   Charlemagne   Napoleon   King Louis XVI

Journal Writing

The French Revolution was started by people in the Third Estate of France. Pretend you are a French peasant in the Third Estate. Write a paragraph that tells why you want a revolution. Give at least two reasons.

Think and Apply

Drawing Conclusions Read each pair of sentences. Then look in the box for the conclusion you might make. Write the letter of the conclusion on the blank.

1. The French people wanted new laws.
The French people decided they did not want another king.

Conclusion _____

2. France spent a lot of money on wars with other nations.
France spent money helping Americans in the American Revolution.

Conclusion _____

3. In 1791 the National Assembly wrote new laws that gave people in France equal rights.
In 1792 the National Assembly said France would not be ruled by a king.

Conclusion _____

4. Marie Antoinette spent large amounts of France's money on items for herself and for her friends.
Marie Antoinette did not seem to care that many people in France were poor and hungry.

Conclusion _____

> **a.** France needed money.
> **b.** The National Assembly helped end absolute rule in France.
> **c.** The French people did not like Marie Antoinette.
> **d.** The French people started a republic.

CHAPTER 23

Napoleon Bonaparte

THINK ABOUT AS YOU READ

1. **How did Napoleon become the ruler of France?**
2. **What changes did Napoleon bring to France?**
3. **How did the Russians defend themselves against Napoleon?**

NEW WORDS

♦ order
♦ Code Napoléon
♦ dictator
♦ censored
♦ defended
♦ allies
♦ allied nations

PEOPLE & PLACES

♦ Russia
♦ Russians
♦ Moscow
♦ Elba
♦ Waterloo
♦ Belgium
♦ St. Helena

Napoleon Bonaparte was a famous leader of the army of France. He became the emperor of France. He won many lands for France. Yet Napoleon died as a prisoner far from home.

Napoleon was born in 1769. His parents came from noble Italian families. Napoleon joined the French army at the age of 16. Later, he became an important leader of the French army.

In 1796 Napoleon led the French army against its enemy, the Austrians. The Austrian army was in northern Italy. The French conquered the Austrians in Italy. Napoleon went on to win other battles. He soon became a famous French hero.

Napoleon wanted to rule France. The government of France was in Paris. In 1799 Napoleon went to the city of Paris with a group of French soldiers. Napoleon and his soldiers forced the leaders of the French

Napoleon Bonaparte carefully planned his attacks on the countries of Europe.

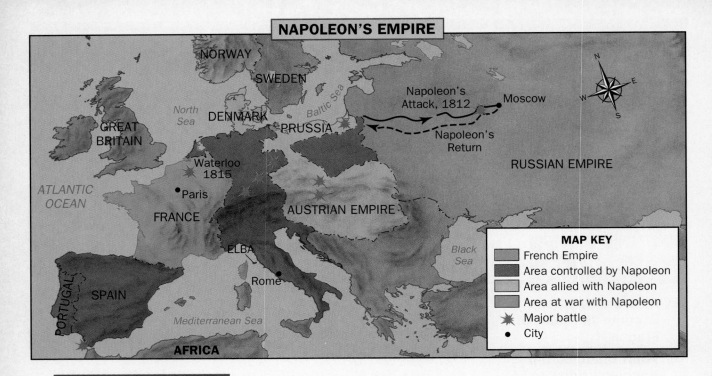

NAPOLEON'S EMPIRE

MAP KEY
- French Empire
- Area controlled by Napoleon
- Area allied with Napoleon
- Area at war with Napoleon
- Major battle
- City

The map shows major battles fought by Napoleon. Which battle took place in the French Empire?

Republic to leave the government. Napoleon became the ruler of France.

The people of France wanted peace. They wanted the French Revolution to end. Napoleon was able to bring **order** to France. He helped solve France's money problems. Under Napoleon's rule, France built many new roads, buildings, and schools.

Napoleon made many fair laws. His system of laws was called the **Code Napoléon**. Some of his laws were based on the goals of the French Revolution. The laws gave religious freedom to all. The laws also said that all French people were equal. All people had to pay taxes.

Napoleon set up a strong French government. He became a **dictator**. A dictator is a ruler who has full power. All the laws of France were made by Napoleon. Napoleon also **censored** newspapers. The newspapers were not allowed to say things against Napoleon. People did not have freedom of speech.

Much of the power of the Roman Catholic Church had been taken from the Church during the French Revolution. In order for the Church to help

Napoleon made himself emperor of France. Here he is crowning his wife empress.

Soldiers of Napoleon

him control France, Napoleon made changes that gave the Church more power. But Napoleon did not return land that was taken from the Church during the French Revolution.

Napoleon wanted more power. So in 1804 Napoleon made himself the emperor of France. As the emperor he ruled all the nations France had conquered. But Napoleon wanted still more power. He wanted to rule all of Europe. He led the French army to war against many countries. By 1810 Napoleon controlled most of Europe. Look at the map of Napoleon's empire on page 156.

Napoleon wanted to conquer Russia. In 1812 he led a large army into Russia. This army had over 400,000 soldiers. Most of the soldiers were from the lands France had already conquered.

The Russians knew that Napoleon was coming. They did not have enough soldiers to win a war against France. They knew they could not defeat Napoleon by fighting. So the Russians **defended** themselves in a different way. They did not want French soldiers to use their homes or to eat their food. The Russians burned their homes and farms. They also burned Moscow, their capital city. They moved into eastern Russia.

Cold winter and snow led to the defeat of Napoleon in Russia.

Napoleon and his soldiers in the burning city of Moscow

Napoleon and his soldiers came to Russia. They found burned cities and burned houses. There were few Russians for the French soldiers to fight. Soon winter came to Russia. There was a lot of snow. The weather was very, very cold. The French soldiers did not have enough food or warm clothing. Napoleon knew he could not conquer Russia. So he decided to return to France with his army. Most of the cold, hungry soldiers died on the way back to France. The Russians and their cold winter had defeated Napoleon.

The conquered people of Europe hated Napoleon. He had forced the conquered people to pay a lot of taxes to France. He had forced conquered men to become soldiers in the French army. The conquered nations learned that Napoleon was defeated in Russia. His army was now very weak. The conquered nations decided to fight to be free again. These and other nations joined together as **allies** in a war against Napoleon. Some of the **allied nations** were Great Britain, Russia, and Austria.

The allied nations invaded France. They captured Paris. In 1814 the allies defeated Napoleon. Napoleon no longer ruled Europe. The allied nations forced Napoleon to leave France. They sent him to a small island called Elba. Elba is near Italy. The allied nations told Napoleon that he could never return to France.

Napoleon was captured by the allies after he lost the battle at Waterloo.

Napoleon on the island of St. Helena

Napoleon escaped from Elba and went back to Paris. He became emperor of France again. He was emperor for only 100 days. In 1815 Napoleon and his soldiers fought the allied nations again at Waterloo. Today Waterloo is a town in the country of Belgium. Find Waterloo on the map on page 156. Napoleon and his soldiers were defeated at Waterloo. Waterloo was Napoleon's last battle. Napoleon became a prisoner of the allies. The allies took Napoleon to St. Helena, a small island near southern Africa. Napoleon died there in 1821.

Napoleon was a strong ruler. He made laws to carry out some of the French Revolution's ideas about democracy. French soldiers spread the idea of "Liberty, Equality, Fraternity" to many parts of Europe. But Napoleon also took away the right to freedom of speech that people had won in the French Revolution. As a dictator and an emperor, Napoleon ruled with full power.

Napoleon had brought years of war to Europe. After Napoleon was defeated, the nations of Europe wanted peace. They wanted Europe to be the way it was before the French Revolution. You will read about Europe after Napoleon in the next chapter.

Using Vocabulary

Finish Up   Choose words in dark print to best complete the sentences. Write the words on the correct blank lines.

defended   allied nations   dictator   censored

1. As _____ of France, Napoleon ruled with complete power.

2. Napoleon _____ newspapers so that they could not say things against him.

3. Instead of fighting Napoleon's soldiers to save Russia, the Russians

   _____ their country by burning their homes and farms.

4. The nations that fought Napoleon were called _____.

Read and Remember

Finish the Paragraph   Use the words in dark print to finish the paragraph below. Write on the correct blank lines the words you choose.

equal   schools   food   Code Napoléon
fight   allies   Europe

   Napoleon became the ruler of France in 1799. He was a strong ruler. Under

Napoleon's rule, new _____ were built in France. The laws made

by Napoleon were called the _____. These laws said that all

French people were _____. Napoleon wanted to rule all of

_____. He tried to conquer Russia, but the French army did

not have enough warm clothing or _____. After that, the other

conquered nations of Europe decided to _____ against

Napoleon. At Waterloo, Napoleon and his soldiers were defeated by the

_____.

Find the Answer   Put a check (✔) next to each sentence that tells something true about Napoleon. You should check four sentences.

_____ **1.** Napoleon was the leader of the French army.

_____ **2.** Napoleon was caught trying to give secrets about France to Austria.

_____ **3.** Napoleon became emperor in 1804.

_____ **4.** Napoleon was a good emperor to all the people he ruled.

_____ **5.** Napoleon took away all of the Roman Catholic Church's power in France.

_____ **6.** In 1812 Napoleon led over 400,000 soldiers into Russia.

_____ **7.** Napoleon died on the island of St. Helena in 1821.

Think and Apply

Categories   Read the words in each group. Decide how they are alike. Find the best title for each group from the words in dark print. Write the title on the line above each group.

Russia   **Waterloo**   **Dictator**   **Allied Nations**

1. _____

Great Britain, Russia, and Austria
defeated Napoleon
took Napoleon to St. Helena

2. _____

censored newspapers
made all laws
had full power

3. _____

burned Moscow
cold winters
burned houses and farms

4. _____

Napoleon's last battle
1815
allies won

Journal Writing

Do you think Napoleon was a good ruler? Write a paragraph to explain your answer.

Europe After Napoleon

As Napoleon conquered more land in Europe, he changed the rulers and the **borders** of the different countries that he had conquered. After Napoleon was defeated, leaders from many European nations met to change again the rulers and the borders in Europe. The leaders met in Vienna, Austria. These meetings were called the **Congress of Vienna**.

The Congress of Vienna began in 1814. It ended in 1815. The leaders of the Congress of Vienna wanted Europe to be the way it was before the French Revolution. They wanted peace. The Congress of Vienna wanted to stop all revolutions. Four important nations led the Congress of Vienna. The four powers were called the **Quadruple Alliance**. Great Britain, Russia, Austria, and Prussia were in the Quadruple Alliance. Later, France joined the Quadruple Alliance.

Leaders met at the Congress of Vienna to make changes in the rulers and the borders of the nations of Europe.

Klemens von Metternich was a leader of the Congress of Vienna. He represented Austria. He was against the ideas of the French Revolution. He thought the ideas of liberty, equality, and fraternity would bring more wars to Europe. He thought that democracy led to wars.

The Quadruple Alliance

Metternich said that only strong kings could keep peace. He wanted all laws to be made by kings. He said people should have less freedom and should not be equal. The other leaders at the Congress of Vienna agreed with Metternich. They began to take away the freedom and the equality that people had won after the French Revolution. The Congress of Vienna helped the old kings become the rulers of their nations again. The old kings again had full power to make all laws in their countries.

The leaders of the Congress of Vienna changed the sizes of some nations in Europe. They did this because they wanted a **balance of power**. A balance of power means that one nation should not be strong enough to conquer other nations. The leaders thought a balance of power would keep peace in Europe. Some nations, such as Russia, became larger. Others became smaller. France lost all land that Napoleon had conquered. The nations around France also became stronger to prevent France from trying to take again the land of other countries.

Klemens von Metternich

Many **secret police** worked for the Quadruple Alliance. They looked for people who might start revolutions. The secret police looked for people who talked against the kings. The people they found were sent to prison. Thousands of people went to prison.

The Congress of Vienna helped Europe in one important way. No big wars were fought for almost forty years. But the Congress of Vienna could not make people forget the ideas of the French Revolution. Europe had many rich merchants in the middle class. These people no longer wanted powerful kings. These people wanted freedom. They wanted to help make their laws. Revolutions began to occur in many European nations.

The first revolutions were in Spain and in northern Italy in 1820. Soldiers from the Quadruple Alliance nations went to Spain and Italy and stopped the revolutions.

Revolution in Austria in 1848

There was also a revolution in Belgium. This revolution was a success. Belgium had been ruled by the Netherlands. The people of the Netherlands are the Dutch. The people of Belgium wanted to rule themselves. In 1830 the people of Belgium fought for their freedom. They fought their Dutch rulers and won. The Quadruple Alliance could not stop this revolution.

In 1830 and in 1848, revolution came again to France. Both times the French forced their king to leave France. In 1848 the French started another republic. The people of France voted for Louis Napoleon to become the president of the Second French Republic. Napoleon Bonaparte had been Louis's uncle. Like his uncle, Louis became a dictator. Later, Louis made himself emperor. By 1870 this new French empire fell apart.

Louis Napoleon

In 1848 revolution came to Austria, where Metternich lived. Angry people began to fight for freedom. Metternich left Austria and went to Great Britain. After that Metternich had no power. The Quadruple Alliance fell apart.

The Congress of Vienna could not stop new revolutions in Europe. The French Revolution had brought new ideas about freedom and equal rights to many parts of Europe. Europe also changed because Europeans learned about the growth of democracy in Great Britain and in America. In the years ahead, people in other parts of the world would also fight for freedom.

Using Vocabulary

Find the Meaning   Write on the blank the word or words that best complete each sentence.

1. **Borders** are the lines that separate _____ .

   people   time periods   nations

2. The **Quadruple Alliance** was a group of nations that included Great Britain,

   Austria, Prussia, and _____ .

   Russia   Spain   Belgium

3. A **balance of power** means that nations have _____ amounts of power.

   equal   different   large

4. The **secret police** were people who looked for other people who might start

   _____ .

   businesses   colonies   revolutions

Read and Remember

Choose the Answer   Draw a circle around the correct answer.

1. Which was Klemens von Metternich against?

   the Congress of Vienna   the ideas of the French Revolution   old kings

2. Which group worked to stop revolutions in Europe?

   merchants   middle class   Quadruple Alliance

3. Which nation did Belgium revolt against in 1830?

   Netherlands   Austria   Russia

4. What did Louis Napoleon rule in 1848?

   Congress of Vienna   Second French Republic   most of Europe

Skill Builder

Reading a Political Map

A **political map** shows how areas of land are divided. Some political maps show how a continent is divided by nations. Thin lines are used to show the borders between nations. Different colors are used to show different nations. Sometimes colors are used more than once. Look at this map of Europe. It shows how Europe was divided after the Congress of Vienna. Study the map. Then write the answer to each question.

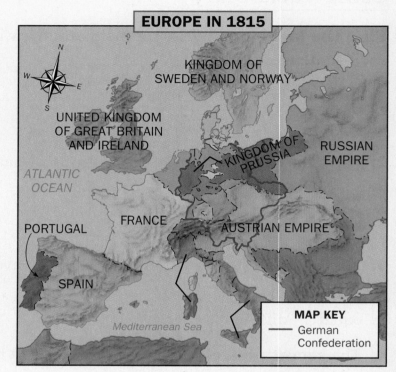

EUROPE IN 1815

KINGDOM OF SWEDEN AND NORWAY

UNITED KINGDOM OF GREAT BRITAIN AND IRELAND

KINGDOM OF PRUSSIA

RUSSIAN EMPIRE

ATLANTIC OCEAN

PORTUGAL

FRANCE

AUSTRIAN EMPIRE

SPAIN

Mediterranean Sea

MAP KEY
— German Confederation

1. What country shares Spain's northeast border?_____

2. Which had more land: the Austrian Empire or the Russian Empire?_____

_____

3. Which were two nations that shared a border with the Austrian Empire?

_____

4. What island nation was located northwest of France?_____

_____

5. What is one nation that has the same color as Portugal?_____

Journal Writing

The Congress of Vienna hoped to bring peace to Europe. Do you think the Congress of Vienna reached this goal? Write a few sentences to explain your answer.

Latin Americans Win Freedom

The countries to the south of the United States are called Latin America. For more than 300 years, Spain ruled most of Latin America. France, Portugal, and some other European nations also held colonies in Latin America. The Latin American colonies were only allowed to trade with their ruling countries. In the 1800s many Latin American colonies wanted to be free of European rule. Latin Americans wanted to rule themselves. They wanted to be able to trade with all nations. They wanted to write their own laws.

Latin Americans knew that American colonists had won their independence from Great Britain during the American Revolution. Latin Americans knew that the French people had fought for their rights during the French Revolution. These two

THINK ABOUT AS YOU READ

1. Why did the people of Latin America decide to fight for freedom?

2. Which people led some of the revolutions in Latin America?

3. How did Brazil become a free country?

PEOPLE & PLACES

- Latin America
- Haiti
- Hispaniola
- Caribbean Sea
- Saint Domingue
- Toussaint L'Ouverture
- Father Miguel Hidalgo
- Mexicans
- José de San Martín
- Simón Bolívar
- Argentina
- Chile
- Peru
- Dom Pedro
- Venezuela
- Bolivia

Father Miguel Hidalgo led Mexico's fight for independence from Spain in 1810.

Slaves in Haiti fought against their French owners and won independence.

Toussaint L'Ouverture

Father Miguel Hidalgo

revolutions helped the people of Latin America decide to fight for their independence.

Haiti is a country on the island of Hispaniola. Hispaniola is in the Caribbean Sea to the north of South America. Haiti is a small Latin American country. It was once a French colony. The French called this colony Saint Domingue. Most of the people in Saint Domingue were slaves on plantations owned by French people. In 1791 a leader of the slaves, Toussaint L'Ouverture, led a revolution against French rule. He was captured by the French in 1799. But the slaves continued to fight. They won the revolution in 1804. They named their new independent country Haiti.

In 1808 Napoleon Bonaparte of France conquered Spain. Napoleon let his brother become the ruler of Spain and of Spain's colonies in Latin America. The people of Latin America did not want to obey a French king. Many Latin Americans decided to fight for their freedom.

Mexico was the first Spanish colony in Latin America to fight to be free. Father Miguel Hidalgo was a Catholic priest in Mexico. He became the leader of Mexico's war against Spain. Father Hidalgo started an army. Most of the soldiers were poor

José de San Martín led an army across the Andes Mountains to help Chile win freedom.

José de San Martín

A Spanish general meets with Simón Bolívar.

American Indians. In 1810 they began to fight. Father Hidalgo and his soldiers won some battles. But in 1811 Father Hidalgo was captured. He was killed by Spanish soldiers. Father Hidalgo became a Mexican hero. But the revolution failed. The Mexicans were not free.

In 1814 the French were driven from Spain. Napoleon's brother no longer ruled Spain. Spain was again ruled by a Spanish king. The Spanish army was weak after fighting against the French. The new Spanish government was weak, too. Because Spain was weak, many Latin American colonies thought they could defeat Spain.

The Mexicans began to fight again for their freedom. In 1821 the Mexicans won their war with Spain. Mexico became an independent nation.

The colonies in South America also wanted to be free. José de San Martín and Simón Bolívar were two great leaders in the fight for freedom in South America. They helped many colonies become independent nations. José de San Martín began the fight for freedom in Argentina. He helped Argentina win its independence from Spain in 1816.

Dom Pedro

MAP KEY
Ruled by Spain
Ruled by Portugal
Other

Independence in Latin America

San Martín decided to also help Chile become free. He formed an army to fight for Chile. The Andes Mountains separated Chile and Argentina. These mountains are some of the tallest mountains in the world. San Martín led his army across the Andes. The trip across the Andes was slow and hard.

At last San Martín and his army came to Chile. The Spanish never thought San Martín would cross the Andes Mountains to fight for Chile. The Spanish soldiers were not ready to fight. San Martín and his army defeated the Spanish. In 1818 Chile became an independent nation. The nations in the southern part of South America were free.

By 1822 Peru was Spain's only colony in South America. It took four more years for this colony to become free. San Martín and Simón Bolívar both fought for freedom in Peru. In 1820 San Martín invaded Peru with his army. He fought there for two years. Then in 1823 Bolívar led the fight for freedom in Peru. Many battles were fought. At last in 1826, Peru became an independent nation. Spain had lost all of its colonies in South America.

Brazil is the largest country in South America. Brazil had been a colony of Portugal. In 1807 Napoleon conquered Portugal. The king of Portugal went to live in Brazil. After Napoleon was defeated, the king went back to Portugal to rule. Dom Pedro, the king's son, became the new ruler of Brazil in 1821.

The people of Brazil wanted to be free. In 1822 Dom Pedro told Portugal that Brazil wanted to rule itself. Portugal did not want to fight against Brazil. Portugal allowed Brazil to be free. Brazil became independent without fighting.

Thousands of people had fought to win freedom for Latin America. By 1826 most of the Latin American colonies had won their freedom. The new nations would work hard to protect their independence. Such freedom is an important part of many nations all over the world.

Simón Bolívar (1783–1830)

Simón Bolívar was born in Venezuela. His parents died when he was young. They left a large amount of money to him. As a young man, Bolívar visited Europe. While in Europe, Bolívar saw the changes brought about by the French Revolution. He read books on freedom by people such as John Locke. In 1805 he made a promise to help Venezuela become a free country.

Bolívar became a leader of the revolutions against the Spanish in Latin America. Bolívar led the fight for freedom in the northern part of South America. He is sometimes called the "George Washington of South America." This is because he helped so many colonies become free. He led the fight for freedom for more than ten years.

Simón Bolívar

Simón Bolívar's army won many battles against the Spanish. He helped free five Latin American nations. One of these nations was Venezuela. In 1823 Bolívar fought to help Peru become independent of Spanish rule. In 1824 one of Bolívar's generals won a major battle that freed most of Peru. Finally in 1826 the defeat of the remaining Spanish army in Peru ended Spanish rule in South America. The northern part of Peru formed a new country called Bolivia. This new country was named after Simón Bolívar.

Simón Bolívar hoped that the new countries in Latin America would become republics. He wanted the people to make their own laws. He hoped that all the countries in Latin America could work together to make Latin America strong. But Bolívar did not ever get to see a united Latin America. Over the years the independent nations would struggle with many problems.

Read and Remember

Write the Answer   Write one or more sentences to answer each question.

1. Why did Latin Americans decide to fight for their independence? _____

_____

2. How did San Martín and his army defeat the Spanish in Chile? _____

_____

_____

3. What happened in 1814 that led to new revolutions in Latin America?

_____

4. Which Latin American country was named after Simón Bolívar? _____

_____

Who Am I?   Read each sentence. Then look at the words in dark print for the name of the person who might have said it. Write on the blank after each sentence the name of the person you choose.

> **Father Miguel Hidalgo**   **Dom Pedro**   **Toussaint L'Ouverture**
> **Simón Bolívar**   **Napoleon**   **José de San Martín**

1. "I led the slaves in the fight for freedom from French rule in Saint Domingue."

_____

2. "I was the French emperor who conquered Spain." _____

3. "My army fought for Mexico's freedom from Spain." _____

4. "I led an army to fight for Chile's freedom." _____

5. "I told Portugal that Brazil wanted to rule itself." _____

6. "Some people have called me the 'George Washington of South America'."

_____

Think and Apply

Understanding Different Points of View   The Spanish and the Latin Americans had different points of view about the fight for independence in Latin America. Read each sentence below. Write **S** next to the sentences that might show the Spanish point of view. Write **LA** next to the sentences that might show the Latin American point of view.

_____ **1.** Spanish kings should rule Latin America.

_____ **2.** Latin Americans should rule themselves.

_____ **3.** Latin American colonies should be able to trade with all countries.

_____ **4.** Spanish colonies in Latin America should trade only with Spain.

_____ **5.** Father Miguel Hidalgo was a hero.

Skill Builder

Reading a Historical Map   The historical map on page 170 shows the dates that different countries in Latin America won their independence. It also shows from which European country each Latin American country won its independence. Study the map and the key. Then answer each question.

1. Which country became independent from Portugal? _____

2. Which nation ruled Chile before 1818? _____

3. Which five countries fought for freedom against Spain? _____

_____

4. Which country was the last to become independent? _____

5. Which country once ruled the country that is now called Haiti? _____

Journal Writing

You have read about many interesting people in world history. Of all the people in this book, whom would you most like to meet? Write a few sentences that explain why you would like to meet this person.

Crossword Puzzle

Each sentence below has a word missing. Choose the missing word for each sentence from the words in dark print. Then write the words in the correct places on the puzzle.

──────────────────── **ACROSS** ────────────────────

Hidalgo   Latin   Argentina   Brazil

1. For more than 300 years, Spain ruled most of _____ America.

2. _____ won its freedom from Portugal without fighting.

3. Father _____ led the fight for freedom in Mexico.

4. José de San Martín began the fight for freedom in _____ .

──────────────────── **DOWN** ────────────────────

Bolívar   Mexico   Chile   Spain

5. Latin America began its fight for freedom when _____ was weak.

6. _____ led the fight for freedom in the northern colonies of South America.

7. In 1818 _____ became a free country.

8. The first Spanish colony to fight for freedom was _____ .

Glossary

absolute rule   page 148
Absolute rule means complete power.

abusing   page 111
A person who is abusing someone is using that person wrongly or is hurting that person.

accused   page 53
An accused person has been charged or blamed for something.

adapted   page 127
A person has adapted to an area if he or she has adjusted to the climate and the natural resources there.

adobe   page 128
Adobe is a mixture of desert clay and straw that is used to make buildings.

agricultural revolution   page 6
The agricultural revolution was a change in the way people got their food.

Allah   page 76
Allah is Islam's name for God.

allied nations   page 158
Allied nations are nations that are united in order to do something.

allies   page 158
Allies are nations that unite in order to do something. Some allies promise to help one another in a war.

alphabet   page 22
An alphabet is the letters used to write a language.

American Revolution   page 142
The American Revolution was the war for freedom that the 13 American colonies fought against Great Britain.

aqueducts   page 54
Aqueducts are bridges or pipes that are used to carry water.

archaeologists   page 4
Archaeologists are people who find and study the bones and tools of people who lived many years ago.

balance of power   page 163
A balance of power means that nations have about the same strength.

barbarians   page 63
Barbarians were groups of people who invaded the Roman Empire.

Bastille   page 149
The Bastille was a prison in Paris. It was captured during the French Revolution.

battles   page 94
Battles are fights between people or groups of people.

Bible   page 25
The Bible is a book of the laws, beliefs, and history of Judaism and Christianity.

bill of rights   page 100
A bill of rights is a list of freedoms and rights of the people of a country.

borders   page 162
Borders are lines that separate countries or other areas.

broken the law   page 100
A person who has broken the law has done something that the law says not to do.

Buddhism   page 31
Buddhism is a religion that was started in India about 500 B.C. by a man called the Buddha.

caravans   page 124
Caravans are groups of people who travel together.

castes   page 31
Castes are groups that Hindus believe people are born into.

caste system   page 31
The caste system was the Hindu way of grouping people into classes.

castles   page 73
Castles were large buildings that nobles built to protect people on the manor.

censored   page 156
A person has censored a newspaper or other item if he or she has refused to let certain information be printed.

china   page 38
China is thin dishes that are made of a fine, white clay.

Christianity page 25
Christianity is a religion that is based on the teachings of Jesus.

citizens page 45
Citizens are people of a city, state, or country.

city-states page 18
City-states are towns or cities that rule themselves and the land around them.

civilization page 10
A civilization is a group of people who have a government and a written language.

civil service system page 39
A civil service system is a system of people who work for the government.

classes page 18
Classes are groups of people who are alike in some way.

Code Napoléon page 156
The Code Napoléon was a system of laws made by Napoleon.

colonies page 44
Colonies are places that are ruled by nations.

colonists page 140
Colonists are people living in a colony.

compass page 117
A compass is an instrument that shows directions.

Congress of Vienna page 162
The Congress of Vienna was a meeting held in 1814 by European leaders.

conquered page 18
A nation or an army that has used force to take control of something has conquered it.

conquerors page 52
Conquerors are people who conquer other people.

Constitution page 144
The Constitution is the laws and the plan of government of the United States.

Counter-Reformation page 113
The Counter-Reformation was the Roman Catholic Church's effort to make people want to stay or to become Catholics.

crescent page 17
A crescent is the thin, curved shape of a moon.

Crusades page 83
The Crusades were wars that Christians and Turks fought in order to control Palestine.

culture page 48
Culture is the way of life of a group of people.

Declaration of Independence page 142
The Declaration of Independence was a paper that said the American colonies were free.

defeat page 99
To defeat means to win a victory over.

defended page 157
When the Russians defended themselves against Napoleon, they protected themselves from an attack by Napoleon.

democracy page 46
A democracy is a kind of government that is run by the people.

dictator page 156
A dictator is a ruler who has all of the power.

diseases page 85
Diseases are sicknesses.

divorce page 113
A divorce is a way to end a marriage by law.

dynasties page 35
Dynasties were groups of kings from the same family. Different dynasties ruled China for thousands of years.

earth page 4
Earth is dirt or soil.

Eastern Orthodox Church page 68
The Eastern Orthodox Church is the part of the Christian church that developed in eastern Europe after the Fall of Rome.

empress page 64
An empress is a female ruler of an empire.

estate page 148
An estate was a class of people in France before the French Revolution.

executed page 94
A person who has been killed because of someone's orders has been executed.

exploration　page 117
Exploration is travel to learn about places.

Fall of Rome　page 63
The end of the Roman Empire in A.D. 476 is called the Fall of Rome.

fertile soil　page 11
Fertile soil is land that is good for crops.

feudalism　page 72
Feudalism was a way of life that helped kings keep their land and people safe.

feudal system　page 72
The feudal system is another term for feudalism.

Five Pillars of Islam　page 77
The Five Pillars of Islam are five duties that Muhammad said Muslims must do.

forgiven　page 112
To be forgiven is to be excused or to not be blamed for something.

freedom of religion　page 134
Freedom of religion is the right to belong to any religious group.

freedom of speech　page 100
Freedom of speech is the right to speak against the government.

French Revolution　page 148
The French Revolution was the war fought by French people to change France's laws and rulers. It lasted from 1789 to 1799.

god　page 11
A god is a person or thing that is considered most important and powerful.

Golden Age　page 49
The Golden Age is the greatest time in the history of a place.

goods　page 83
Goods are things that are bought and sold.

guilty　page 53
To be guilty means to have done something wrong.

Hinduism　page 31
Hinduism is the main religion in India. Hindus believe in many gods.

holy　page 82
Holy means special for religious reasons.

honest　page 24
To be honest means to tell the truth.

House of Commons　page 100
The House of Commons is the group in Parliament that is made up of middle-class people.

House of Lords　page 100
The House of Lords is the group in Parliament that is made up of nobles.

Hundred Years' War　page 94
The Hundred Years' War was a war that was fought between England and France from 1337 until 1453.

independent　page 142
To be independent is to be free from another's control. An independent country rules itself.

indulgences　page 112
Indulgences were papers that were sold by the Roman Catholic Church. These papers said a person was forgiven for the wrong things he or she had done.

innocent　page 53
To be innocent means to have done nothing wrong.

invaded　page 36
People have invaded a place if they have attacked the place in order to rule it.

irrigate　page 11
To irrigate means to bring water to dry land.

irrigation　page 30
Irrigation is when water is brought to dry land so that the land will grow crops.

Islam　page 76
Islam is the religion started by Muhammad. People who believe in Islam are Muslims.

isolation　page 93
Isolation is when something is set apart from the rest of a group.

Judaism　page 23
Judaism is the religion of the Jews. Judaism has one God.

jury   page 100
A jury is a group of people who are chosen to decide about something after hearing the facts about it.

knights   page 72
Knights were soldiers during the Middle Ages who fought for nobles and kings.

Koran   page 77
The Koran is the book of Muhammad's teachings.

"Liberty, Equality, Fraternity"   page 150
"Liberty, Equality, Fraternity" was a phrase said by people in the French Revolution. The words meant that people wanted freedom and equal rights.

literature   page 104
Literature is writing. Plays, stories, and books are different types of literature.

Magna Carta   page 99
The Magna Carta was a paper that said the king of England must obey laws.

manor   page 72
A manor was the land a noble ruled.

merchant   page 83
A merchant is a person who buys things and then sells them to make money.

Middle Ages   page 71
The Middle Ages were the years from the Fall of Rome in 476 to about 1500.

middle class   page 100
The middle class is the group of people between the rich and the poor.

monarchs   page 92
Monarchs are kings and queens.

monarchy   page 93
A monarchy is a nation ruled by a king or queen.

monks   page 32
Monks are men who study a religion and follow special rules.

mosques   page 79
Mosques are places where Muslims pray to Allah.

movable type   page 107
Movable type is metal letters that can be put in different orders to make words. Movable type can be used to print books.

National Assembly   page 149
The National Assembly was a group of people who made new laws for France during the French Revolution.

nations   page 92
Nations are groups of people who have the same laws and leaders. People in a nation often speak the same language.

New Testament   page 67
The New Testament is the part of the Bible that tells about Jesus and his teachings.

New World   page 119
People in Europe called the Americas the New World because they had not known about these continents.

95 Theses   page 112
The 95 Theses was Martin Luther's list of statements about the wrong things that the Roman Catholic Church was doing.

nobles   page 72
Nobles were rich people in the feudal system of the Middle Ages.

Old Testament   page 25
Early stories about the Jews are in the part of the Bible called the Old Testament.

order   page 156
Order in a nation means that people obey laws and rules.

outcastes   page 31
Outcastes are people who do not belong to any group in the Hindu caste system.

Parliament   page 100
Parliament is the group of people who make laws for Great Britain.

patriarch   page 68
The patriarch is the head of the Eastern Orthodox Church.

peace treaty   page 143
A peace treaty is a promise between nations to not fight against one another.

peasants   page 73
Peasants are people who work on farms. In the feudal system, the peasants worked for the nobles.

peninsula   page 44
A peninsula is an area of land that has water on almost all sides.

pharaohs   page 11
Pharaohs were rulers of ancient Egypt.

pilgrimage   page 77
A pilgrimage is a trip to a place that is special for the members of a religion.

plague   page 64
A plague is a very serious sickness that spreads quickly and kills many people.

plantations   page 133
Plantations are large farms where many people work to grow crops for the owner.

pope   page 68
The pope is the head of the Roman Catholic Church.

population   page 62
Population is the number of people who live in a place.

priests   page 18
Priests are religious leaders.

prison   page 99
A prison is a place where people who have broken the law are forced to live.

prophet   page 76
A prophet is a person who believes that God has spoken to him or her. A prophet tells other people what God said.

pyramids   page 12
Pyramids were large stone buildings that the people of ancient Egypt built for their rulers' tombs.

Quadruple Alliance   page 162
The Quadruple Alliance was a group of four nations that worked together to stop revolutions in Europe after 1814.

Ramadan   page 77
Ramadan is a special month during which Muslims do not eat or drink during the day.

raw materials   page 132
Raw materials are things that have not been changed from their natural form. Many raw materials are grown or dug from the earth.

rebirth   page 104
Rebirth means something is born again. The Renaissance was a rebirth of art and learning.

reborn   page 31
To be reborn means to be born again as a new person or another living creature.

recaptured   page 83
To have recaptured something means to have taken control of it again.

Reformation   page 111
The Reformation was a movement to make changes in the Catholic Church.

regions   page 127
Regions are large areas of a country or a continent.

religion   page 23
A religion is a belief in a god or gods.

religious   page 105
Religious means having to do with religion.

Renaissance   page 104
The Renaissance was a time when learning and creating became important in Europe. The Renaissance began about 1300 and lasted about 300 years.

representatives   page 141
Representatives are people chosen to speak or act for others.

republic   page 52
A republic is a nation that is not ruled by a king or queen.

respected   page 37
To be respected means to be shown honor and to be treated well by others.

riots   page 64
Riots are large crowds of angry people that fight and make noise.

Roman Catholic Church   page 68
The Roman Catholic Church is the part of the Christian church that developed in western Europe after the Fall of Rome.

royal   page 150
Royal means having to do with kings or queens.

ruling countries   page 132
Ruling countries are countries that rule colonies.

sacrifice   page 126
To sacrifice means to offer something to a god in order to please the god. The Aztecs sacrificed people by killing them.

scarce   page 17
Something that is scarce is hard to find or get.

Scientific Revolution   page 106
The Scientific Revolution was a time in which people made many inventions and discoveries. The Scientific Revolution began during the Renaissance.

secret police   page 163
Secret police are people who pretend not to be police so that they can find people who are against the government.

Senate   page 53
The Senate is a group of elected leaders in a republic.

senators   page 53
Senators are members of the Senate. They are leaders who make laws.

silk   page 38
Silk is a soft, shiny cloth that was first made by the Chinese.

slaves   page 13
Slaves were people who were owned by other people. They did hard work without pay and could not leave their owners.

soldiers   page 36
Soldiers are members of an army who fight for and guard a nation.

spices   page 85
Spices are seeds or other parts of plants that add different tastes to food.

Stamp Act   page 141
The Stamp Act was a British law that forced Americans to pay a tax on printed items, such as newspapers.

Stone Age   page 4
The Stone Age is the time when most people used stone tools. The Stone Age began more than 2,000,000 years ago.

Sugar Act   page 141
The Sugar Act was a law that forced Americans to pay taxes to Great Britain on certain goods brought to the 13 colonies.

tame   page 6
To tame means to make a wild animal gentle and easy to handle.

taxes   page 61
Taxes are money that people pay to the government.

temple   page 14
A temple is a building in which people worship a god or gods.

Ten Commandments   page 24
The Ten Commandments are laws that tell people how to behave. Jews and Christians believe that God gave these laws to Moses.

tombs   page 12
Tombs are graves or buildings where the bodies of the dead are placed.

tools   page 4
Tools are objects that help people do work.

trading posts   page 134
Trading posts were stores where people could exchange food and supplies.

trial   page 53
A trial is a meeting to decide whether an accused person has broken the law.

veto   page 53
A veto is a government leader's power to stop a new law from being passed.

voyage   page 118
A voyage is a long journey by water or through space.

weapons   page 14
Weapons are objects that are used to attack or to protect something.

woodblock printing   page 84
Woodblock printing is a way to make books using letters or symbols carved in wood.

PHYSICAL MAP OF THE WORLD

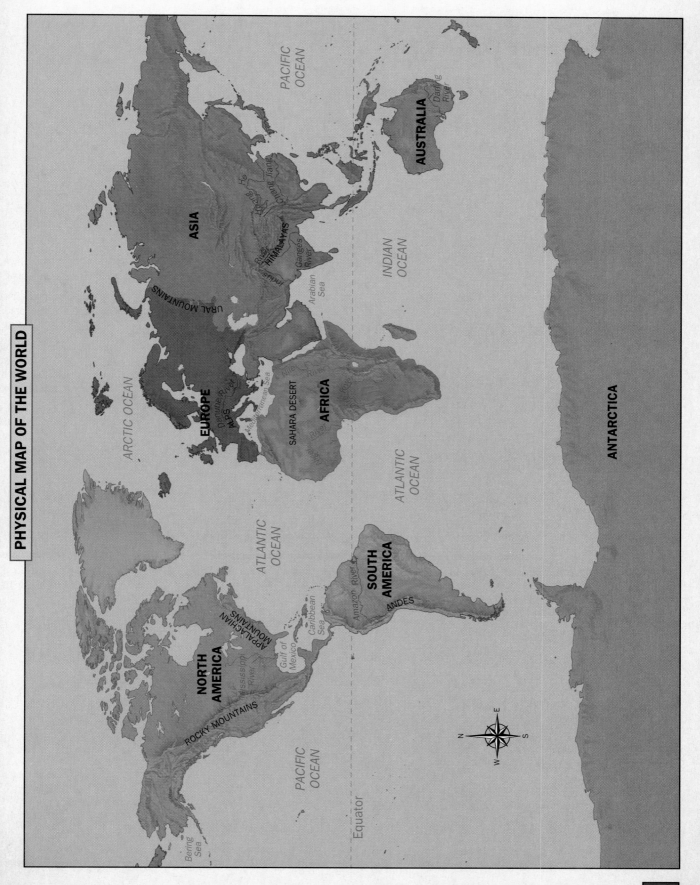

Time Line

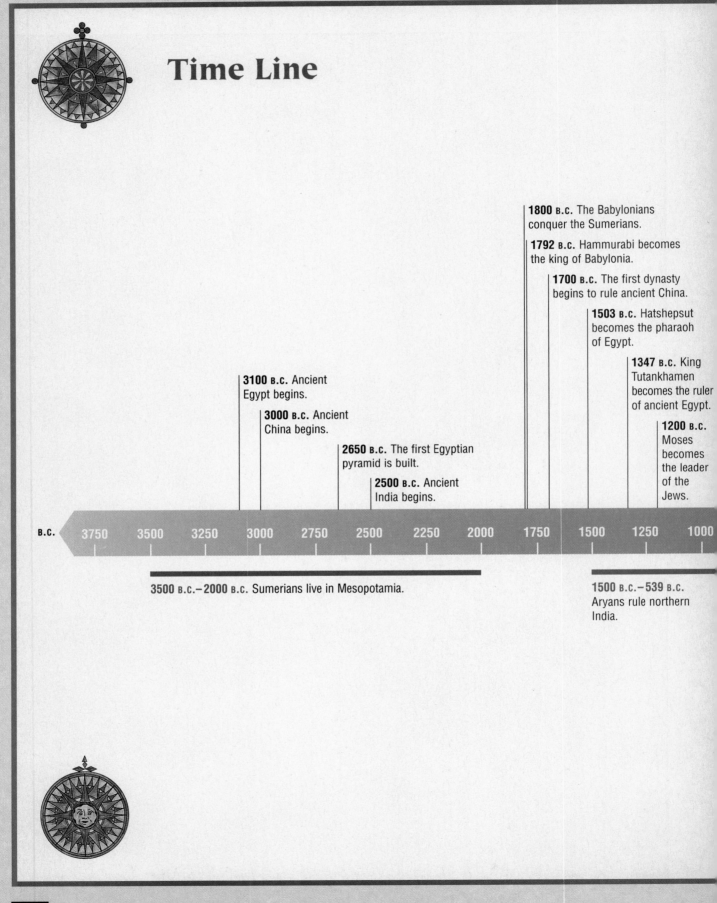

3100 B.C. Ancient Egypt begins.

3000 B.C. Ancient China begins.

2650 B.C. The first Egyptian pyramid is built.

2500 B.C. Ancient India begins.

1800 B.C. The Babylonians conquer the Sumerians.

1792 B.C. Hammurabi becomes the king of Babylonia.

1700 B.C. The first dynasty begins to rule ancient China.

1503 B.C. Hatshepsut becomes the pharaoh of Egypt.

1347 B.C. King Tutankhamen becomes the ruler of ancient Egypt.

1200 B.C. Moses becomes the leader of the Jews.

B.C. | 3750 | 3500 | 3250 | 3000 | 2750 | 2500 | 2250 | 2000 | 1750 | 1500 | 1250 | 1000

3500 B.C.–2000 B.C. Sumerians live in Mesopotamia.

1500 B.C.–539 B.C. Aryans rule northern India.

753 B.C. Ancient Rome begins.

551 B.C. Confucius is born.

539 B.C. Persians conquer Babylon.

508 B.C. Athens becomes a democracy.

500 B.C. Buddhism begins.

323 B.C. Alexander the Great dies.

221 B.C. People of ancient China begin building the Great Wall.

202 B.C. Han Dynasty begins to rule ancient China.

49 B.C. Julius Caesar becomes the leader of Rome.

0 Jesus is born.

14 Augustus Caesar dies.

180 The Roman Empire's 200 years of peace end.

476 The Roman Empire falls.

527 Justinian and Theodora become rulers of the Byzantine Empire.

622 Muhammad flees to Mecca.

1000 Ghana is a strong empire. Zimbabwe is built.

1071 The Turks capture Jerusalem.

1200 The Aztec and Inca empires begin.

1295 Marco Polo returns to Italy from China.

1307 Mansa Musa becomes the king of Mali.

1453 France wins the Hundred Years' War.

1519 Magellan sails around South America.

1689 The English Bill of Rights is written.

1776 Americans write the Declaration of Independence.

1789 The French Revolution begins.

1814 Napoleon is defeated. The Congress of Vienna meets.

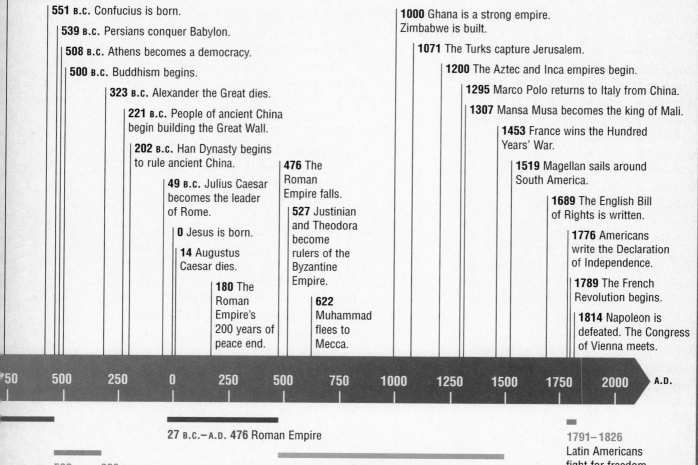

| 750 | 500 | 250 | 0 | 250 | 500 | 750 | 1000 | 1250 | 1500 | 1750 | 2000 | A.D. |

27 B.C.–A.D. 476 Roman Empire

539 B.C.–330 B.C. Persians rule a large empire.

A.D. 476–1500 Middle Ages in Europe

1791–1826 Latin Americans fight for freedom from European rule.

1095–1291 Crusades

1200–1700 Growth of democracy in England

1300–1600 Renaissance in Europe

Index